Contents

Tables

Figures

1. Summary

Recorded Crime

1.1 The 62,222 notifiable offences recorded by the police in 1997 represented a 9% decrease compared to 1996 and is the lowest level of recorded crime since 1990 (57,198). Theft is the single largest offence group accounting for 47% of all recorded crime in 1997. A total of approximately £45.7 million of cash and property was stolen in 1997 by way of theft, burglary, robbery, and fraud & forgery, less than the previous year (£47.5 million).

Crime Trends

1.2 There were decreases in eight of the nine recorded crime categories in 1997 compared to 1996. Theft fell by 3,229 offences (down 10%); burglary by 1,808 offences (down 11%); violence against the person was down 486 offences, a decrease of 9%; recorded sex offences fell by 17% (down 301 offences); fraud and forgery fell by 6% (a decrease of 263 offences); offences of criminal damage dropped 155 offences (down 3%); and other notifiable offences (mainly drug offences) fell by 9% (down 114 offences); robbery offences fell by 4% (down 72 offences). Offences against the state increased by 101 offences (up 25%) - mainly due to an increase in recorded public order offences.

Crime Clear-up

1.3 In 1997 there were 19,560 notifiable offences cleared by the police. This is a 15% decrease compared to the number cleared in 1996 and represents an overall clear-up rate of 31% in 1997. This is the second consecutive annual decrease in the clear-up rate and the lowest rate recorded in the last ten years. Comparing 1997 with 1988 the clear-up rates were 31% and 45% respectively.

1.4 Offence groups which typically demonstrate high clear-up rates are other offences (mainly drug offences), sexual offences, offences against the state, violence against the person and offences involving fraud or forgery. Rates for 1997 are 89%, 86%, 78%, 59% and 56% respectively. Approximately one quarter of theft and one quarter of criminal damage offences were cleared up. Offences which have the lowest clear-up rates both currently and historically are burglary (18%) and robbery (16%).

Court Proceedings

1.5 In 1997 the number of defendants proceeded against at magistrates' courts was 34,471, a 1% decrease on 1996. Total prosecutions for summary and indictable offences (14,238) fell by 5% in 1997 compared to 1996 (15,029). Motoring prosecutions increased in 1997 by 2% to 20,233. Most prosecutions in magistrates' courts have been against adult males (85% in 1997).

1.6 There were 1,128 prosecutions in the Crown Court in 1997, 6% less than 1996. This is the second successive annual fall and the 1997 figure is 24% less than in 1988 (1,486). Most persons prosecuted in 1997 (1,027) were adult males (91%).

Court Outcomes

1.7 In 1997 86% of defendants at the magistrates' court and 88% of defendants at the Crown Court pleaded guilty. Of those pleading not guilty, 85% in magistrates' courts and 63% in Crown Courts were acquitted. In 1997, 53% of those convicted in all courts had at least one previous conviction. In terms of gender the highest rate of conviction in 1997 was for males aged 19 years and females aged 18 years.

1

Sentencing

1.8 In the Crown Court, the most frequently used disposal is immediate custody. This was given to 590 offenders in 1997 - 57% of those found guilty. A further 27% (280) received a suspended custodial sentence, and 8% (84) were given supervision in the community. Immediate custody continues to be given more frequently for those convicted of scheduled offences. In 1997, 68% of scheduled offenders received immediate custody.

1.9 In magistrates' courts, a fine is the most common disposal, being given in 1997 to 71% of all offenders - 28% of those convicted of indictable offences, 48% of those convicted of summary offences, and 92% of those convicted of motoring offences. Immediate custodial sentences are much less frequently used than in the Crown Court - 5% of all disposals in 1997 - reflecting the less serious nature of the offences dealt with. The rate for the Crown Court in 1997 was 57%.

1.10 In 1997 there were 955 juveniles sentenced by the courts, 700 for indictable offences, 198 for summary offences, and 57 for motoring offences. 180 juveniles were sentenced to immediate custody (most being sent to a training school) in 1997 constituting 19% of all juvenile disposals. Supervision in the community (41%); the conditional discharge (25%) and immediate custody (19%) are the most common disposals given to juveniles found guilty at all courts in 1997.

The Prison Population

1.11 In 1997 the average prison population fell for the fourth consecutive year to 1,632 - a very slight decrease compared to 1996 and a fall of 14% compared to 1988.

1.12 A comparison of the 1997 and 1996 average prison populations shows that the number of males and females are basically unchanged - an average of 1,610 males in 1996 compared to 1,602 in 1997 and an average of 29 females in 1996 compared to 30 in 1997. Overall prisoners sentenced to immediate custody have fallen by 4% from 1,278 in 1996 to 1,226 in 1997. Fine default prisoners have increased from an average of 24 in 1996 to 30 in 1997 and remand prisoners have increased by 12% from an average of 326 in 1996 to 366 in 1997.

1.13 Prison receptions increased marginally between 1996 (5,498) and 1997 (5,502). There were increases in both fine default (up 8%) and in non-criminal receptions (up from 27 in 1996 to 42 in 1997) counterbalanced by a 3% decrease in immediate custody prisoner receptions and a 5% decrease in remand receptions. Overall in 1997, 40% of receptions were remand prisoners, 34% were fine defaulters and 25% were sentenced to immediate custody and 1% were non-criminal prisoners.

1.14 In 1997 52% of the average prison population sentenced to immediate custody had committed offences of violence against the person, 13% offences of dishonesty (theft, fraud & forgery, burglary), 10% offences of robbery, 9% sexual offences, 8% drug offences, and 3% criminal damage offences.

2. Notifiable offences recorded by the Police

Introduction

2.1 The recording process for crime normally starts when someone reports to the police that an offence has been committed, when the police discover an offence, or when an offender asks for further offences to be taken into consideration. The police make an initial examination of the facts to determine if there is prima facie evidence that an offence has been committed, and if so a crime report may be filed. If this is the case, and the offence is a serious one, and is contained in a list of notifiable offences prepared by the Home Office, the offence may be recorded for statistical purposes. Less serious offences such as motoring offences, liquor law offences and cruelty to animals are noted by the police and processed without being recorded for statistical purposes.

Counting Rules

2.2 In recording offences the Royal Ulster Constabulary (RUC) broadly follow Home Office counting rules, issued to ensure as much comparability as possible of figures from different areas and over time. Inevitably some variation does occur. The statistics on notifiable offences incorporate <u>each offence as initially recorded</u>, which may differ from the one for which a suspect or suspects are finally proceeded against. Some offences consist of continuous or repetitive activity; in other cases several people may be the victim of the same criminal act; while some criminal acts may involve the infringement of a number of distinct parts of the criminal law. The Home Office rules specify that, except in special circumstances, only the most serious offence is counted where several offences are committed in one incident. The most serious offence is that which would incur the greatest penalty. Where there was a finding of guilt, the principal offence is usually that for which the greatest penalty was imposed. An exception is made for offences of violence against the person and sexual offences where there is more than one victim, when one offence is usually counted for each victim. Another important concept of the rules is that in the case of a continuous series of offences where there is some special relationship, knowledge or position existing between the offender and the person or property offended against which enables the offender to repeat the offences, only one offence is counted for each continuous offence.

Coverage

2.3 The coverage and categorisation of 'notifiable offences recorded' in this commentary is similar to that of 'notifiable offences' recorded by police forces in England and Wales. An outline of the offences included in each main category, together with an indication of how these differ from those used in England and Wales, is given in Appendix 1. A specific difference from Home Office practice is that criminal damage offences involving under £200 are not recorded in Northern Ireland. All cases, irrespective of the amount involved, are in theory recordable in England and Wales, though this is not always done for cases involving less than £20.

2.4 From 1988 'communication of false information causing a bomb hoax' and 'assault on a constable' are no longer included as notifiable offences, in line with Home Office practice. Data for earlier years have been revised accordingly.

The Extent of Recording

2.5 Offences recorded by public bodies such as the Post Office Investigation Branch, and DHSS are not included, unless they have also been reported to the RUC, or have come to their notice as a result of court proceedings where the defendant may have asked for the offence to be taken into consideration. Prosecutions undertaken by the Department of the Environment in respect of motor tax offences and by the Television Licensing Authority in respect of licence offences are also excluded.

2.6 Statistics of crime recorded by the RUC provide a measure of the amount of crime with which they are faced, but only a partial picture of crime committed. Evidence on the extent of under-reporting is available from victim surveys such as the British Crime Survey (Great Britain), General Household Survey (Great Britain), the Continuous Household Survey (Northern Ireland), the 1996 International Crime Victims Survey and the Northern Ireland Crime Survey. These generally indicate that the propensity to report crime is influenced by a number of factors such as offence severity, whether a suspect is known to the victim, the ease with which a report can be made, insurance claim requirements, public attitudes to the police, public attitudes to certain offences (e.g. sexual offences), changes in legislation etc. The British Crime Survey suggests that "incomplete reporting and recording mean that only just over a quarter [of comparable crimes]... are estimated to end up in police records"[1]. In general under-reporting is most prevalent for less serious crime with the most serious crimes, such as murder, generally being known to the police. Because the influence of the several factors may vary over time, trends in the number of recorded crimes may differ from trends in the number of crimes committed. Changes in recorded crime, and particularly small year-on-year changes, need to be interpreted with caution.

Recorded Crime

2.7 At 62,222, the number of recorded offences in 1997 decreased by nine percent (down 6,327 offences) on the 1996 level (68,549) (Table 2.1). This is the lowest level of recorded crime since 1990 (57,198).

Figure 2.1: NOTIFIABLE OFFENCES RECORDED BY THE POLICE 1988-1997

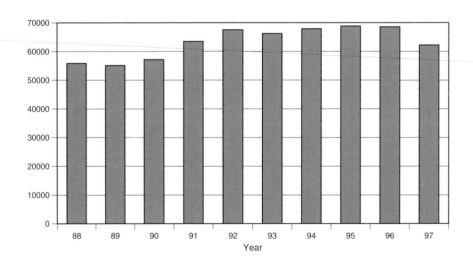

[1] Source: 'Trends in Crime: Findings from the 1994 British Crime Survey' (Pat Mayhew, Catriona Mirrlees-Black and Natalie Aye Maung), Research Findings No.14, Home Office Research and Statistics Department, 1994.

2.8 There were decreases in eight of the nine recorded crime categories in 1997 compared to 1996. Theft fell by 3,229 offences (down 10%); burglary by 1,808 offences (down 11%); violence against the person was down 486 offences, a decrease of 9%; recorded sex offences fell by 17% (down 301 offences); fraud and forgery fell by 6% (a decrease of 263 offences); offences of criminal damage dropped 155 offences (down 3%); other notifiable offences (mainly drug offences) fell by 9% (down 114 offences); and robbery offences fell by 4% (down 72 offences). Offences against the state increased by 101 offences (up 25%) - mainly due to an increase in recorded public order offences.

Figure 2.2: NOTIFIABLE OFFENCES RECORDED BY CRIME CATEGORY 1997

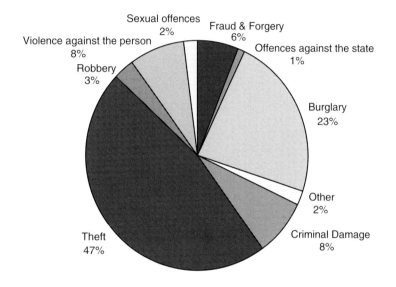

Violence against the Person

2.9 The number of offences of violence against the person in 1997 decreased on the previous year to 5,154 (a decrease of 9% on 1996). The 1997 figure is 49% higher than that recorded in 1988 (3,469). Figure 2.3 shows that murders in 1997 increased to 40 from 35 in 1996; attempted murders also rose from 71 to 116. The main decrease was in assault offences such as wounding/grievous bodily harm/assault occasioning actual bodily harm which fell by 12% (down 535 offences) on the 1996 figure.

Figure 2.3: NOTIFIABLE OFFENCES OF MURDER AND ATTEMPTED MURDER 1988-1997

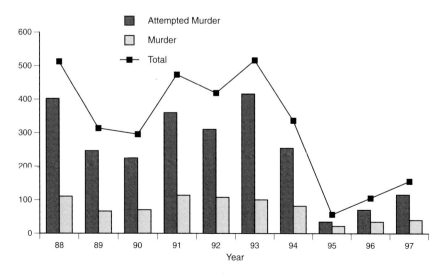

5

2.10 Sexual offences recorded in 1997 fell to 1,444, a decrease of 17% over the previous year (1,745). The 1997 level is nearly twice that for 1988 (779). Within the category of sexual offences the number of indecent assaults fell with 793 offences recorded during 1997, 20% down on the figure for the previous year (991). This was the first decrease in recorded offences of indecent assault in the last decade. There was a slight increase in the number of rapes recorded in 1997 (268) compared to 1996 (264). This increase, combined with a slight decrease in the number of attempted rapes means that the 1996 (292) and 1997 (294) rape-related crime figures are similar.

Figure 2.4: NOTIFIABLE OFFENCES OF RAPE[1] AND INDECENT ASSAULT 1988-1997

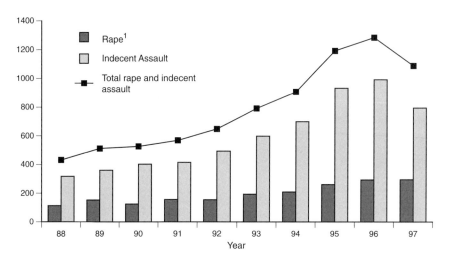

[1] Includes attempts.

2.11 Burglary fell to 14,306 recorded offences in 1997, an 11% decrease from the 1996 level of 16,114. The 1997 level is similar to that recorded in 1988 (14,353) (see Figure 2.5). More burglaries in 1997 occurred in dwellings (7,435) than in non-dwellings (6,717). Recorded offences of burglary in a dwelling fell by 1,095 offences (down 13%) in 1997 and burglary in a non-dwelling fell by 10% (down 709 offences). All burglaries accounted for £10.4 million of stolen property and cash in 1997.

Figure 2.5: NOTIFIABLE OFFENCES OF BURGLARY 1988-1997

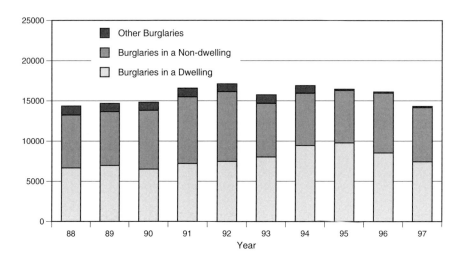

2.12 There were 1,653 robberies recorded in 1997, representing a decrease of 4% from the 1,725 recorded in 1996 and a decrease of 22% on the 1988 level (2,130). The number of hijackings increased for the third year in a row rising by 25% from 439 in 1996 to 548 in 1997 whilst recorded armed robbery fell by 5% from 655 in 1996 to 621 in 1997. All robberies accounted for £4.5 million of stolen property and cash in 1997.

Figure 2.6: NOTIFIABLE OFFENCES OF ROBBERY 1988-1997

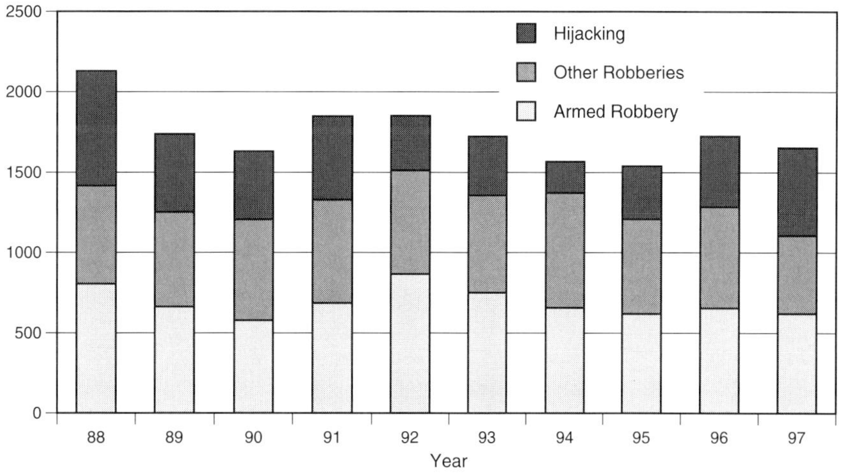

Theft

2.13 There were 29,543 thefts recorded in 1997, a decrease of 10% on the 1996 level (32,772). This is the first time since 1990 (29,267) that recorded theft has been below 30,000 crimes. The 1997 level is 6% higher than that for 1988 (27,994). Theft from motor vehicles (5,416) fell by 1,138 offences and is 17% less than in 1996 (6,554). The 1997 figure is the lowest recorded in the last 10 years. Theft or unauthorised taking of motor vehicles increased (8,633) by 229 offences (up 3%) on 1996 (8,404) and is the fourth highest figure recorded in the last decade. Shoplifting offences (4,501) fell for the second consecutive year (down 17% on 1995 - 5,410 offences) but is still 15% higher than the 1988 level (3,920). £28.5 million of property and cash was stolen by way of theft in 1997, a similar amount to the previous year.

Figure 2.7: NOTIFIABLE OFFENCES OF THEFT 1988-1997

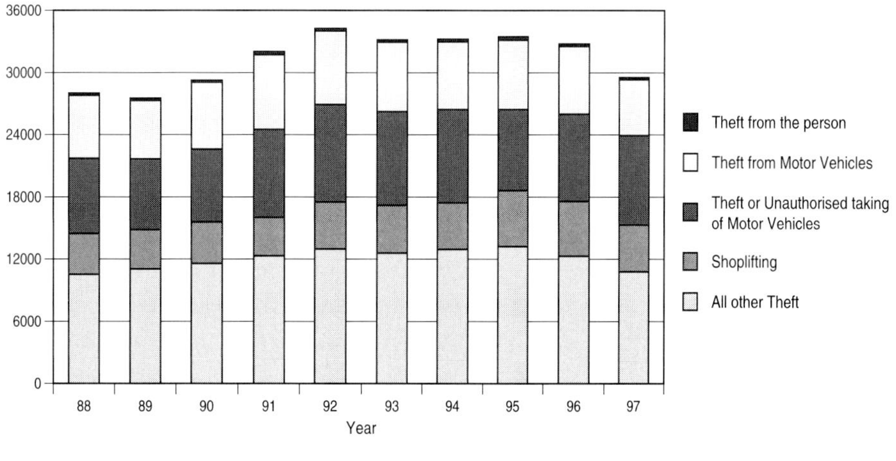

7

2.14 Offences of fraud and forgery recorded by the police fell in 1997 to 3,818, a fall of 6% on 1996 (4,081). This is the fourth successive annual decrease and the 1997 figure is 31% less than that for 1993 (5,553) and is similar to that in 1988 (3,881). Since 1996 the number of forgery offences (374) fell slightly to stand at 357. The number of frauds also fell (by 7%) compared to the number recorded in 1996. Within the frauds category the number of deception offences fell by 20% (down 542 offences) from 2,677 to 2,135 whilst the number of offences of making off without payment increased by 29% from 991 to 1,279. The financial cost of these offences in 1997 was £2.2 million.

Figure 2.8: NOTIFIABLE OFFENCES OF FRAUD AND FORGERY 1988-1997

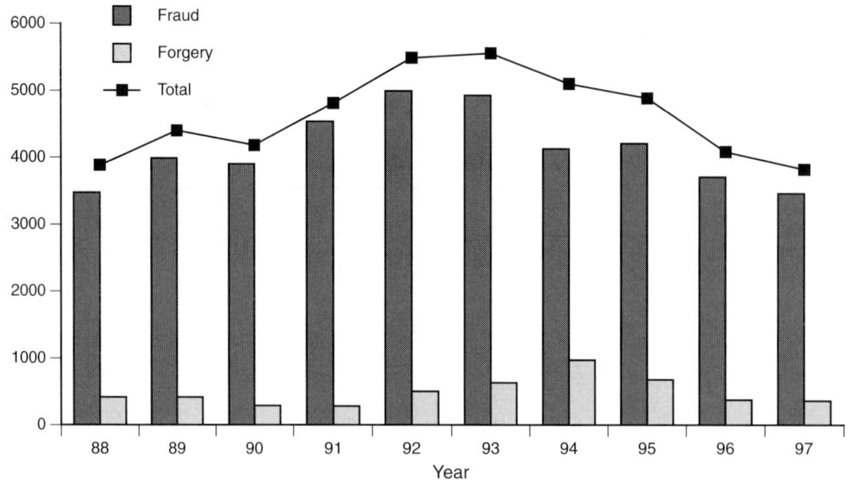

2.15 There were 4,692 offences of criminal damage recorded in 1997. This is a 3% decrease on the 1996 level (4,847) and represents the first annual decrease since 1989 (2,013). The 1997 figure is still the second highest level recorded in the last decade. The peak was 1996 (4,847) and the 1997 level is over twice that for 1988 (2,254). Arson which accounted for approximately one third of all criminal damage offences in 1996 (1,490) decreased numerically for the first time in 1997 (1,201) since 1989 (682) accounting for approximately one quarter of all offences in 1997.

2.16 There were 501 offences against the state recorded in 1997, a 25% increase on the 1996 figure of 400. The 1997 figure is 22% less than the 1988 level (644). The 1988 figure was the highest recorded during the last 10 years. Other offences against public order have increased in recent years and the 1997 figure (414) is 122 offences (42% higher) up on the 1996 figure (292). This offence category is not the sole quantification of terrorist-type offences which may also be found under other headings (e.g. violence against the person and robbery).

2.17 In the category of 'other notifiable offences' (including kidnapping, drug offences and false imprisonment) in 1997, 1,111 offences were recorded by the police, a 9% decrease on the previous year (1,225). This decrease was largely due to a second annual decrease in the number of recorded drug offences from 1,426 in 1995 to 1,093 in 1996 (a decrease of 23%) then to 998 in 1997 (a fall of 9%) - an overall decrease of 30% in the last 2 years. Despite recent decreases the 1997 figure (998) is still over four times that of 1988 (232).

2.18 Police records show that £45.7 million worth of property and cash was stolen in 1997, compared to £47.5 million in 1996.

Figure 2.9: THE VALUE OF PROPERTY AND CASH STOLEN IN 1997 BY OFFENCE CATEGORY

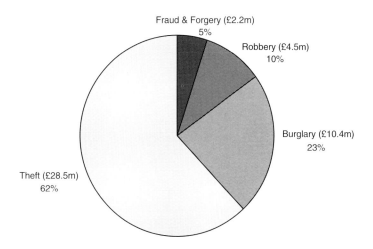

2.19 The value of property and cash stolen in the last ten years peaked at £55.5 million in 1994 before decreasing to £43.9 million in 1995 (a 21% reduction). The 1997 figure is 4% higher than that for 1995.

Figure 2.10: THE VALUE OF PROPERTY AND CASH STOLEN 1988-1997

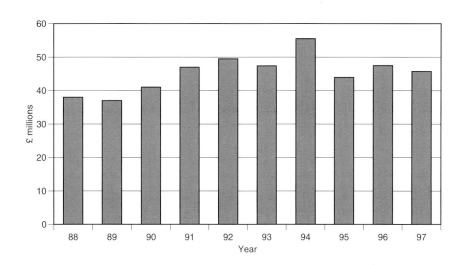

2.20 Table 2.2 shows crime rates per 100,000 population in Northern Ireland and England and Wales over the decade 1988-1997, based on offences defined as 'crime index' offences in the United States of America. This index excludes fraud, criminal damage and offences against the state which are normally included in data for Northern Ireland. On this basis the aggregate crime rate in Northern Ireland for the seven offence categories included in the crime index is less than in England and Wales. Compared to England and Wales, Northern Ireland has a higher rate of homicide and rape (including attempted rape) but lower rates in all other categories.

TABLE 2.1: Notifiable offences recorded by the police 1988-1997

CRIME CATEGORY	1988	1989	1990	1991	1992	1993	1994	1995	1996	1997
VIOLENCE AGAINST THE PERSON	**3469**	**3338**	**3374**	**3955**	**4102**	**4597**	**4793**	**5150**	**5640**	**5154**
Murder	111	67	71	114	108	101	82	22	35	40
Manslaughter & infanticide	5	8	11	7	3	5	4	2	4	2
Attempted murder	402	247	225	360	311	416	255	35	71	116
Other violence against the person	2951	3016	3067	3474	3680	4075	4452	5091	5530	4996
SEXUAL OFFENCES	**779**	**935**	**790**	**877**	**973**	**1187**	**1333**	**1679**	**1745**	**1444**
Rape	94	109	94	117	116	151	168	229	264	268
Attempted rape	20	43	31	38	38	42	40	30	28	26
Incest	34	24	38	25	35	20	24	13	15	4
Indecent assault	317	359	401	413	493	597	698	932	991	793
Other sexual offences	314	400	226	284	291	377	403	475	447	353
BURGLARY	**14353**	**14680**	**14817**	**16563**	**17117**	**15735**	**16902**	**16457**	**16114**	**14306**
Burglary in a dwelling	6655	6967	6505	7206	7461	8005	9454	9774	8530	7435
Burglary in a building other than a dwelling	6583	6691	7311	8281	8677	6675	6480	6499	7426	6717
Other burglary [1]	1115	1022	1001	1076	979	1055	968	184	158	154
ROBBERY	**2130**	**1738**	**1630**	**1848**	**1851**	**1723**	**1567**	**1539**	**1725**	**1653**
Armed robbery	805	663	579	686	866	751	657	620	655	621
Hijacking	713	487	425	519	339	365	194	331	439	548
Other robbery	612	588	626	643	646	607	716	588	631	484
THEFT	**27994**	**27057**	**29267**	**32033**	**34256**	**33161**	**33233**	**33472**	**32772**	**29543**
Theft from the person	219	220	219	304	242	217	257	330	235	201
Theft in a dwelling	587	472	428	304	356	436	427	618	628	559
Theft from motor vehicles	6058	5626	6443	7227	7117	6729	6555	6715	6554	5416
Theft or unauthorised taking of motor vehicles	7272	6386	7042	8455	9376	9011	8974	7794	8404	8633
Shoplifting	3920	3780	3984	3737	4549	4625	4510	5410	5291	4501
Other thefts	9938	10573	11151	12006	12616	12143	12510	12605	11660	10233
FRAUD & FORGERY	**3881**	**4395**	**4177**	**4811**	**5486**	**5553**	**5100**	**4884**	**4081**	**3818**
Frauds	3471	3983	3895	4533	4991	4922	4127	4204	3707	3461
Forgery	410	412	282	278	495	631	973	680	374	357
CRIMINAL DAMAGE	**2254**	**2013**	**2191**	**2394**	**2502**	**2856**	**3077**	**3772**	**4847**	**4692**
Arson	773	682	691	805	860	901	940	1132	1490	1201
Explosives offences	97	81	90	112	117	88	65	13	7	21
Other criminal damage [2]	1384	1250	1410	1477	1525	1867	2072	2627	3350	3470
OFFENCES AGAINST THE STATE	**644**	**626**	**585**	**592**	**478**	**436**	**440**	**339**	**400**	**501**
Offences under the NI Emergency Provisions Act	124	150	133	151	103	87	106	18	61	32
Firearms offences	178	175	119	114	73	76	98	42	47	55
Other offences against the state	342	301	333	327	302	273	236	279	292	414
OTHER NOTIFIABLE OFFENCES	**386**	**365**	**367**	**419**	**767**	**980**	**1441**	**1516**	**1225**	**1111**
Drug offences	232	219	216	287	619	811	1286	1426	1093	998
Other notifiable offences	154	146	151	132	148	169	155	90	132	113
GRAND TOTAL	**55890**	**55147**	**57198**	**63492**	**67532**	**66228**	**67886**	**68808**	**68549**	**62222**

Notes: (1) From 1995 excludes 'Attempted burglary' which is included in 'Burglary in a dwelling' or 'Burglary in a building other than a dwelling'.

(2) Other criminal damage excludes offences where damage was under £200.

TABLE 2.2: Crime index offence categories 1988-1997: rate per 100,000 population

	Year	Homicide[1]	Rape[2]	Robbery [3]	Aggravated Assault	Burglary	Larceny Theft	Motor Vehicle Theft[4]
Northern Ireland	1988	7	7	90	212	910	1313	461
	1989	5	10	79	206	927	1306	403
	1990	5	8	76	207	932	1398	443
	1991	8	10	83	239	1034	1472	528
	1992	7	10	93	247	1058	1537	579
	1993	6	12	83	275	964	1480	552
	1994	5	13	84	287	1030	1478	547
	1995	1	16	73	311	998	1557	473
	1996	2	18	77	337	969	1465	505
	1997	3	18	66	306	856	1251	516
England & Wales	1988	1	6	62	312	1620	3099	726
	1989	1	7	65	348	1630	3195	776
	1990	1	7	71	362	1979	3696	972
	1991	1	8	89	371	2386	4265	1139
	1992	1	8	103	392	2643	4419	1142
	1993	1	9	112	397	2663	4198	1152
	1994	1	10	116	423	2437	3930	1024
	1995	1	10	132	418	2401	3776	971
	1996	1	12	142	459	2239	3650	934
	1997	1	13	123	483	1946	3384	765

Notes: (1)   Includes Murder, Manslaughter and Infanticide - excludes attempts.
   (2)   Includes Attempted Rape.
   (3)   Excludes Hijacking.
   (4)   Excludes Theft from vehicles.
   (5)   Population estimates and projections may be revised leading to slight changes in rates per 100,000 population.

3. Offences cleared by the Police

Introduction

3.1 Broadly an offence, having been recorded for statistical purposes, is said to be cleared if a person has been charged, summonsed, or cautioned for the offence; if the offence is 'taken into consideration' by the court; if there is sufficient evidence to charge a person but the case is not proceeded with because, for example, the suspected offender is under the age of criminal responsibility; or if the suspected offender has died. Because the 'clear-up rate' is conventionally taken as the ratio of offences cleared in a year to the offences recorded in the year and some offences cleared will have been recorded in previous years, clear-up rates may occasionally exceed 100%. They vary considerably for different offences and changes in the overall rate for a major offence category may be due to changes in the proportion of sub-categories within that group. Clear-up rates may also vary because of the nature of the offence. Some offences of violence against the person and some sexual offences have high clear-up rates because the victim can more often readily identify the offender. In the case of some fraud offences the discovery of the offence may identify the offender.

Overall Clear-up

3.2 There were 19,560 notifiable offences cleared by the police in 1997. This represents a decrease of 15% (-3,543) on the 23,103 crimes cleared in 1996 and is the lowest number of crimes cleared in the last 10 years. The clear-up rate at 31% is three percentage points less than that of 1996 and is the lowest overall clear-up rate recorded in the last 10 years. Clear-up rates peaked in the last decade at a record high of 45% in 1988 (25,226) after which they fell and remained constant at 36% during the 1993-1995 period before declining to the 1997 rate of 31%.

Figure 3.1: NUMBER OF CRIMES CLEARED AND AS A PERCENTAGE OF CRIMES RECORDED 1988-1997

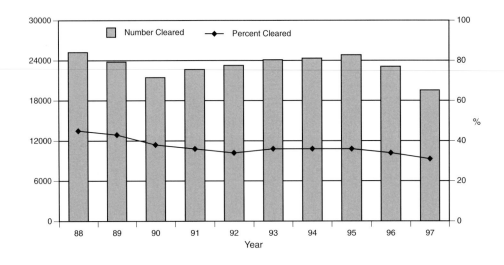

3.3 Trends in clear-up rates for individual categories of crime can be seen in Table 3.1.

Offence Types

3.4 Offence groups which typically demonstrate high clear-up rates are other offences (mainly drug offences), sexual offences, offences against the state, violence against the person and offences involving fraud or forgery. Rates for 1997 are 89%, 86%, 78%, 59% and 56% respectively.

12

Figure 3.2: CRIMES CLEARED (NUMBER AND CLEAR-UP RATE): OTHER NOTIFIABLE OFFENCES 1988-1997

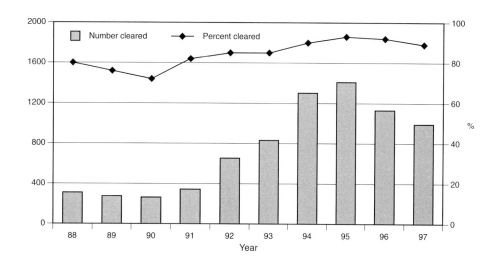

Figure 3.3: CRIMES CLEARED (NUMBER AND CLEAR-UP RATE): SEXUAL OFFENCES 1988-1997

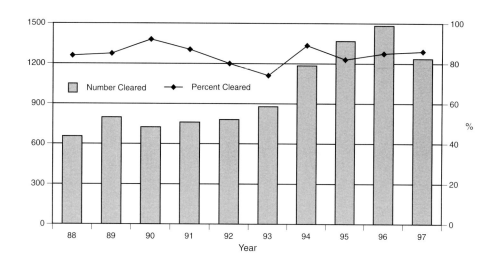

Figure 3.4: CRIMES CLEARED (NUMBER AND CLEAR-UP RATE): OFFENCES AGAINST THE STATE 1988-1997

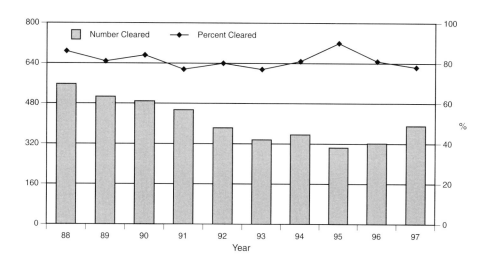

Figure 3.5: CRIMES CLEARED (NUMBER AND CLEAR-UP RATE): VIOLENCE AGAINST THE PERSON 1988-1997

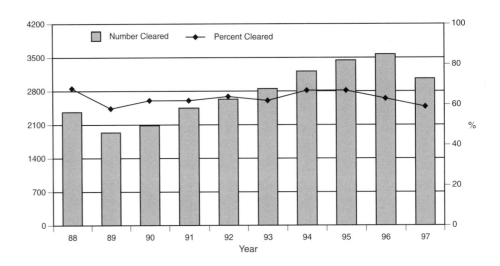

Figure 3.6: CRIMES CLEARED (NUMBER AND CLEAR-UP RATE): FRAUD AND FORGERY 1988-1997

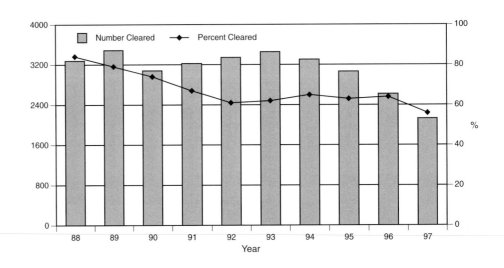

3.5 Clear-up rates for recorded crime tend to vary considerably depending on the nature of the offence. Broadly speaking the clear-up rate tends to be low where the victim can less easily identify the offender. Such offences include criminal damage, theft, burglary and robbery.

3.6 Offences which are currently and historically less successfully cleared up are recorded criminal damage and theft. The clear-up rate for criminal damage rose slightly in 1997 (28%) but is at its second lowest rate of clear-up in the last 10 years. The 1997 clear-up rate for theft (26%) is the lowest rate in the last decade, having fallen steadily from a decade high of 45% in 1988.

14

Figure 3.7: CRIMES CLEARED (NUMBER AND CLEAR-UP RATE): CRIMINAL DAMAGE 1988-1997

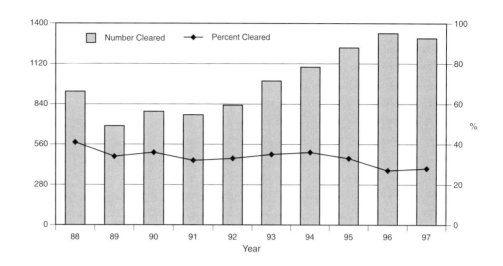

Figure 3.8: CRIMES CLEARED (NUMBER AND CLEAR-UP RATE): THEFT 1988-1997

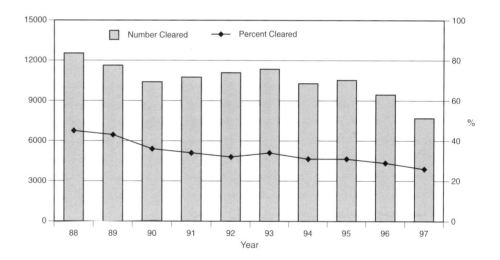

3.7 Offences which have the lowest clear-up rates both currently and historically are burglary and robbery. The clear-up rate for burglary (18%) in 1997 is the joint lowest rate in the 1988-1997 period (18% in 1996) and is more than ten percentage points lower than the rate in 1988 (29%). Over the last ten years there has been a steady decline in the clear-up rate for burglary offences. The clear-up rate for robbery in 1997 (16%) is the same as the 1996 rate which was the second lowest rate in the last ten years. Robbery clear-up rates have ranged from a low of 15% in 1993 to a high of 23% in 1988 during the 1988-1997 period.

Figure 3.9: CRIMES CLEARED (NUMBER AND CLEAR-UP RATE): BURGLARY 1988-1997

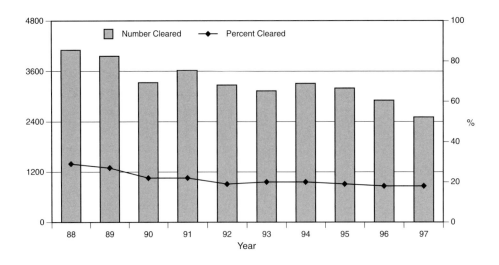

Figure 3.10: CRIMES CLEARED (NUMBER AND CLEAR-UP RATE): ROBBERY 1988-1997

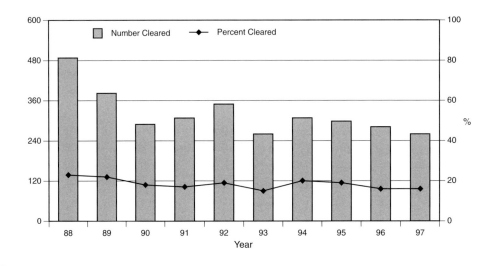

Comparative Trends
in Crime Clear-up

3.8 The Northern Ireland clear-up rate was 45% in 1988, four successive decreases resulted in it falling to 34% in 1992 but rising to 36% in 1993 and it remained the same for 1994 and 1995. The rate fell in 1996 to 34% - the same as the 1992 level before falling to 31% in 1997. There has been a narrowing of the gap between the clear-up rates in Northern Ireland and those in England and Wales in recent years. The clear-up rate in England and Wales was 35% in 1988 before five successive annual decreases resulted in it falling to 25% in 1993. The rate rose to 26% during 1994, 1995, and 1996 before rising to 28% in 1997.

3.9 A comparison of the actual number of crimes cleared between Northern Ireland and England and Wales shows that from 1996 to 1997 there was a 15% decrease in the number of crimes cleared in Northern Ireland (23,103 falling to 19,560) compared to a 2% decrease in England and Wales (1.29 million falling to 1.26 million). In Northern Ireland the 1997 clear-up rate of 31% was equalled or bettered by 20 police forces in England and Wales (out of 43 police force areas) compared to 7 out of 43 police force areas in 1996 when the Northern Ireland clear-up rate was 34%.

3.10 A comparison of how crimes are cleared up between Northern Ireland and England and Wales over the 1988-1997 period illustrates differences in clear-up methods. In England and Wales the proportion of crimes cleared up through individuals being charged peaked at 53% in 1989 before four successive decreases to 45% in 1993. It has remained around this rate during 1993-1996 (falling to 44% in 1995) before two successive rises to 46% in 1997. The rate for Northern Ireland is typically higher although again has shown a reduction in recent years falling from 59% in 1989 and 1990 to 49% in 1996, which was the lowest rate recorded in the last 10 years. The 1997 rate was 51%.

3.11 In both jurisdictions the proportionate rates of clear-up by the use of cautioning also provide interesting comparisons. In England and Wales the proportion remained constant at 11% between 1988-1991. Between 1992 and 1997 the rate ranged between 13% and 15% the mode being 14%. The 1997 rate was 14%. In Northern Ireland the rate gradually increased from 8% to 16% during the 1988-1996 period. In 1997 the proportion cleared up via cautioning fell from 16% the previous year to 9%.

3.12 The use of the "taken into consideration" method as a way of clearing crime has reduced in both jurisdictions over the last 10 years. From a peak of 18% of all crimes cleared in 1991 the rate in England and Wales has fallen to 10% and has been at this level during the 1995-1997 period. The rate of decrease in Northern Ireland has been even more marked with the rate peaking in 1988 at 16% before steadily falling to 3% in 1997.

3.13 Comparing the two jurisdictions in 1997, it would appear that more crimes are cleared in Northern Ireland (51%) by way of charging than in England and Wales (46%) and that England and Wales makes more use of the caution (14%) and the "taken into consideration" method (10%) than in Northern Ireland where the rates are 9% and 3% respectively.

Figure 3.11: CRIMES CLEARED IN 1997 BY METHOD OF CLEARANCE

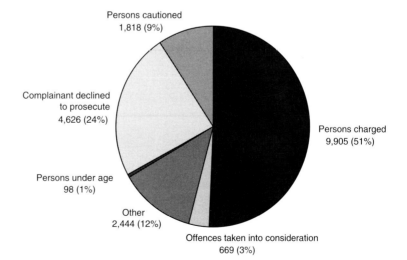

3.14 In Northern Ireland an increasing proportion of crimes are being cleared up because the complainant has declined to prosecute. The rate of crimes being cleared by this method has steadily increased from 11% of crimes cleared in 1988 to a peak of 24% in 1997. A small but constant percentage (1%) of all crimes cleared in Northern Ireland over the last 10 years have been because the person has been under age.

TABLE 3.1: Crimes recorded and crimes cleared by the police 1988-1997

CRIME CATEGORY	1988	1989	1990	1991	1992	1993	1994	1995	1996	1997
Notifiable crimes recorded	55890	55147	57198	63492	67532	66228	67886	68808	68549	62222
Number of crimes cleared	25226	23808	21475	22675	23253	24088	24342	24838	23103	19560
Clear-up rate (%)	45	43	38	36	34	36	36	36	34	31

TABLE 3.2: Notifiable offences cleared by the police as a percentage of those recorded 1988-1997

CRIME CATEGORY	1988 (%)	1989 (%)	1990 (%)	1991 (%)	1992 (%)	1993 (%)	1994 (%)	1995 (%)	1996 (%)	1997 (%)
VIOLENCE AGAINST THE PERSON	**68**	**58**	**62**	**62**	**64**	**62**	**67**	**67**	**63**	**59**
Murder	71	45	28	60	51	52	58	64	63	65
Manslaughter & infanticide	100	50	109	43	200	160	75	100	125	0
Attempted murder	46	24	28	27	34	35	31	74	49	34
Other violence against the person	71	61	65	66	67	65	69	67	63	60
SEXUAL OFFENCES	**84**	**85**	**92**	**87**	**80**	**74**	**89**	**82**	**85**	**86**
Rape	74	90	88	80	80	76	69	83	81	79
Attempted rape	50	67	77	97	71	81	73	70	79	88
Incest	103	92	89	84	106	80	71	115	87	100
Indecent assault	84	82	89	83	73	80	82	81	80	82
Other sexual offences	88	89	100	94	90	63	112	82	98	97
BURGLARY	**29**	**27**	**22**	**22**	**19**	**20**	**20**	**19**	**18**	**18**
Burglary in a dwelling	25	23	20	18	16	15	16	18	17	17
Burglary in a building other than a dwelling	27	28	22	21	19	22	22	19	17	16
Other burglary (1)	62	54	44	54	46	43	43	98	99	97
ROBBERY	**23**	**22**	**18**	**17**	**19**	**15**	**20**	**19**	**16**	**16**
Armed robbery	22	24	20	18	17	14	18	17	19	22
Hijacking	23	17	13	9	24	13	22	10	5	4
Other robbery	23	26	19	21	19	18	21	27	21	21
THEFT	**45**	**43**	**36**	**34**	**32**	**34**	**31**	**31**	**29**	**26**
Theft from the person	25	26	23	24	17	19	16	15	23	19
Theft in a dwelling	62	61	65	54	57	66	63	57	54	44
Theft from motor vehicles	22	21	14	12	9	10	8	10	8	7
Theft or unauthorised taking of motor vehicles	46	46	31	29	27	30	19	18	15	14
Shoplifting	100	88	89	92	85	83	86	83	80	74
Other thefts	36	37	31	31	29	31	30	28	26	24
FRAUD & FORGERY	**84**	**79**	**74**	**67**	**61**	**62**	**65**	**63**	**64**	**56**
Frauds	84	78	74	68	43	64	71	66	66	58
Forgery	84	87	77	52	63	45	38	39	46	39
CRIMINAL DAMAGE	**41**	**34**	**36**	**32**	**33**	**35**	**36**	**33**	**27**	**28**
Arson	25	24	22	20	22	19	20	18	12	14
Explosives offences	38	31	37	33	12	31	26	62	29	24
Other criminal damage (2)	51	40	43	38	41	43	43	39	34	33
OFFENCES AGAINST THE STATE	**86**	**81**	**84**	**77**	**80**	**77**	**81**	**90**	**81**	**78**
Offences under the NI Emergency Provisions Act	102	95	97	101	97	95	90	167	84	91
Firearms offences	84	79	84	73	79	66	59	52	66	47
Other offences against the state	82	75	78	67	75	74	86	91	82	81
OTHER NOTIFIABLE OFFENCES	**80**	**76**	**72**	**82**	**85**	**85**	**90**	**93**	**92**	**89**
Drug offences (3)	*	*	*	99	92	91	93	94	97	93
Other notifiable offences	80	76	72	47	58	57	70	74	54	54
GRAND TOTAL	**45**	**43**	**38**	**36**	**34**	**36**	**36**	**36**	**34**	**31**

Notes:
(1) From 1995 excludes 'Attempted burglary' which is included in 'Burglary in a dwelling' or 'Burglary in a building other than a dwelling'.
(2) Other criminal damage excludes offences where damage was under £200.
(3) Drug offences not available separately prior to 1991 - included in Other notifiable offences.

4. Court Proceedings

Introduction

4.1 Most persons suspected by the police of having committed an offence are prosecuted. This chapter considers the number of defendants proceeded against at certain stages of the criminal justice process.

4.2 Proceedings in the criminal courts start in a court of summary jurisdiction. Adults appear in a magistrates' court where less serious cases are dealt with by way of summary hearing or trial. More serious cases are committed for trial to the Crown Court, if the Magistrate is satisfied there is a case to answer. Juveniles aged 10-16 normally appear first in a special juvenile court of summary jurisdiction, which is empowered to deal with a wider range of offences than the corresponding adult court. Further details of the operation of criminal courts in Northern Ireland are given in Appendix 2.

4.3 The statistics are based on returns made by the RUC on those defendants against whom proceedings were completed in the appropriate year. Although care is taken in completing and analysing the returns, the detail collected is subject to the inaccuracies inherent in any large scale recording system, and to variation in recording practice over time. The coverage is restricted to those prosecutions in which the RUC is involved, excluding prosecutions brought by certain government departments, public bodies and private individuals.

Types of Offences

4.4 Offences are referred to as either indictable, summary or "triable-either-way" essentially depending on whether the case against an adult defendant must be heard at the Crown Court, magistrates' court, or under certain circumstances may be heard at either. For convenience all triable-either-way offences are now included under the heading 'indictable', irrespective of how the case was dealt with. In respect of years prior to 1986, some triable-either-way offences were counted as summary if dealt with in a magistrates' court. The scope and categorisation of offences referred to as indictable are explained in Appendix 1 and under "triable-either-way" offences in Appendix 2.

4.5 Offences can be further classified as scheduled or non-scheduled depending on whether or not they are included in Schedule 1 of the Northern Ireland (Emergency Provisions) Act 1991. Scheduled offences are those typically committed by terrorists. In the Crown Court scheduled offences are dealt with in special non jury courts. The Attorney General has the power to "de-schedule" offences appearing in Schedule 1 where there was no act of terrorism involved e.g. a domestic murder. These and non-scheduled offences are processed through the normal Crown Court jury system. The Attorney General also has the power to certify certain scheduled offences as being suitable for summary trial in magistrates' courts. The most significant example is the offence of Assault Occasioning Actual Bodily Harm (AOABH). The statistics of scheduled offences in this chapter refer only to those heard in the Crown Court.

Counting Rules

4.6 The offence shown in the tables is one for which the court took its final decision. This is not necessarily the same as that for which the defendant was initially proceeded against. The decision recorded is that reached by the court and takes no account of any subsequent appeal to a higher court. If a number of defendants are jointly charged with a particular offence, each is recorded, as are any charges dealt with on separate occasions. Where proceedings involve more than one offence dealt with at the same time, the tables record only the principal offence. The basis for selection of the principal offence is laid down in rules issued by the Home Office. In summary these indicate that, where there is a finding of guilt, the principal offence is usually that for which the greatest penalty was imposed. Where there has not been a finding of guilt (e.g. on acquittal or committal for trial on all charges) it is usually that for which the greatest penalty could have been imposed.

4.7 Most proceedings are against individuals, but a few are against companies. Because the numbers are small they have not been shown separately and by convention are included with figures for adult males.

Magistrates' Courts

4.8 In 1997 the number of defendants proceeded against at magistrates' courts was 34,471, a 1% decrease on 1996. Total prosecutions for summary and indictable offences (14,238) fell by 5% in 1997 compared to 1996 (15,029). Motoring prosecutions increased in 1997 by 2% to 20,233.

4.9 Most prosecutions in magistrates' courts have been against adult males (85% in 1997). In 1997, 29,326 adult males were proceeded against compared with 4,031 adult females, 994 male juveniles and 120 female juveniles. The number of juveniles (1,114) proceeded against fell for the first time since 1992 and overall has fallen by 15% since 1988 (1,317).

Figure 4.1: MAGISTRATES' COURTS PROSECUTIONS BY AGE GROUP AND GENDER 1988-1997

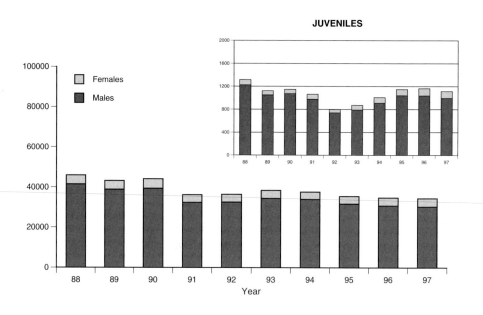

4.10 The offence classifications for adult and juvenile prosecutions show a marked difference (see Figure 4.2). In the case of adults 60% were motoring offences, 24% indictable, and 16% summary. In contrast 74% of juvenile prosecutions were indictable offences, 21% summary, and 6% motoring.

**Figure 4.2: ADULT AND JUVENILE PROSECUTIONS AT MAGISTRATES'
COURTS IN 1997 BY OFFENCE CLASSIFICATION**

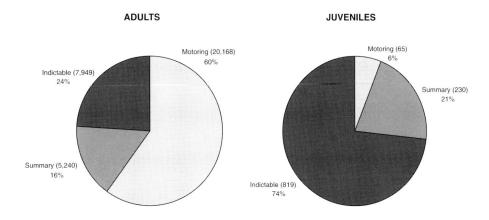

Percentages may not add to 100 due to rounding.

4.11 A comparison of adult and juvenile prosecutions for more serious indictable offences indicates that whilst adults are more likely to be prosecuted for offences of violence against the person (22%) than juveniles (7%), the most common type of offence leading to prosecution for both adults and juveniles is theft accounting for 48% of all juveniles and 33% of all adult prosecutions.

**Figure 4.3: ADULT AND JUVENILE INDICTABLE OFFENCE
PROSECUTIONS AT MAGISTRATES' COURTS IN 1997
BY CRIME CATEGORY**

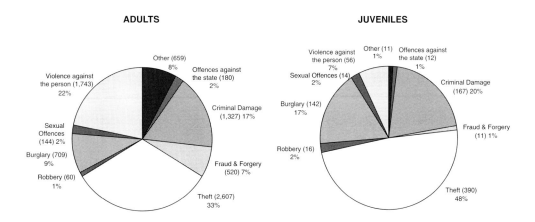

Percentages may not add to 100 due to rounding.

4.12 There were 1,128 prosecutions in the Crown Court in 1997, 6% less than 1996. This is the second successive annual fall and the 1997 figure is 24% less than in 1988 (1,486). Most prosecutions in 1997, 1,027 (91%), were adult males; of the remainder 79 were adult females, 21 were male juveniles and one was a female juvenile.

Figure 4.4: CROWN COURT PROSECUTIONS BY SCHEDULED STATUS 1988-1997

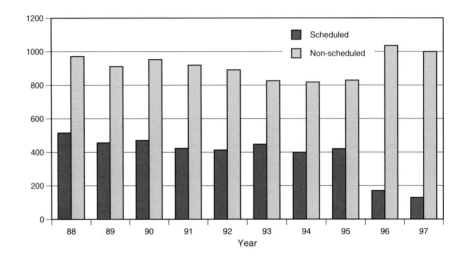

4.13 The 129 prosecutions for scheduled offences was 24% less than the previous year (170). The level of prosecutions for non-scheduled offences fell for the first time since 1994 and is similar to the 1988 level (971).

4.14 Most defendants plead guilty, whether in magistrates' court or the Crown Court, and whether charged with indictable, summary or motoring offences. In 1997 86% of defendants at the magistrates' court and 88% of defendants at the Crown Court pleaded guilty and as a consequence most cases resulted in a guilty finding. In magistrates' courts in 1997, 18% of defendants were found not guilty of indictable offences, 19% not guilty of summary offences and 7% not guilty of motoring offences. In the Crown Court 8% of defendants were acquitted.

4.15 Of those pleading not guilty a sizeable proportion are acquitted. In the magistrates' courts in 1997 of 4,763 pleading not guilty, 4,054 (85%) were acquitted. In the Crown Court of the 141 pleading not guilty, 89 (63%) were acquitted.

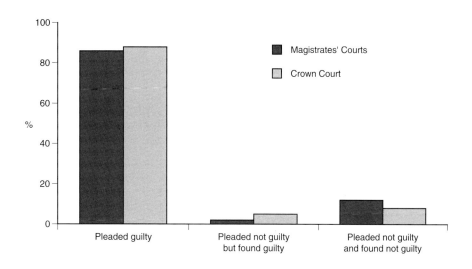

Persons Convicted by Age and Gender

4.16 The number of offenders found guilty in relation to the population is shown in Figure 4.6 and in Table 4.11. Because a person found guilty on two or more separate occasions during the year is counted more than once, the rates shown over-estimate the proportion of the population who are known offenders in any one year. Overall the rate of conviction in 1997 was 219 per 10,000 population. The rate for females, at 48 per 10,000, is considerably less than that for males at 400 per 10,000. In 1997 the rate of conviction was highest for males aged 19 years and females aged 18 years.

Figure 4.6: **RATE OF CONVICTION BY AGE AND GENDER 1997**

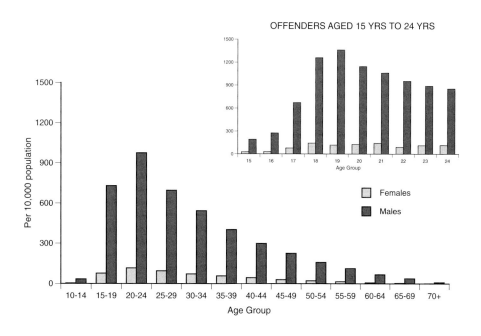

Figure 4.7: JUVENILE PLEAS AND FINDINGS AT ALL COURTS 1997

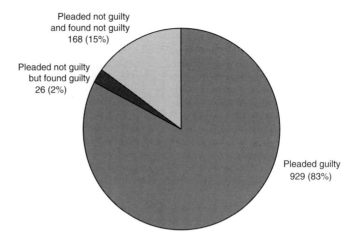

4.17 Of the 1,123 juvenile prosecutions in 1997 with an outcome, 83% (929) of all juveniles initially pleaded guilty. 26 (2%) of those who pleaded not guilty were actually found guilty. 168 (15%) of all juvenile prosecutions with an outcome resulted in an acquittal. Only 2% (22) of all juvenile prosecutions with an outcome in 1997 were in the Crown Court. Of these, 3 pleaded not guilty. Overall 20 juveniles were convicted.

Previous Convictions

4.18 Of all those found guilty in 1997 (excluding companies and public bodies) 53% had previous convictions and the percentage is higher for males (56%) than females (33%). Figure 4.8 shows that previous convictions are more likely for males convicted at the Crown Court (67%) than for females (37%). This pattern is repeated in the magistrates' courts where males are more likely to have previous convictions after a 1997 conviction for an indictable (62%), summary (53%), or motoring offence (57%) than females (49%, 25% and 39% respectively).

Figure 4.8: PERCENTAGE OF THOSE FOUND GUILTY IN 1997 HAVING A PREVIOUS CONVICTION BY GENDER, COURT TYPE AND OFFENCE CLASSIFICATION

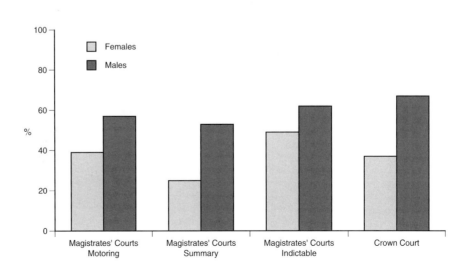

24

TABLE 4.1: Magistrates' courts: Persons proceeded against by principal offence and gender (Adults and Juveniles) 1988-1997

CRIME CATEGORY		1988	1989	1990	1991	1992	1993	1994	1995	1996	1997
Violence against the person	Male	1512	1509	1856	1735	1658	1690	1568	1790	1711	1625
	Female	106	132	162	136	143	142	129	147	183	174
Sexual offences	Male	246	248	291	213	189	136	173	241	232	153
	Female	1	3	0	3	1	2	1	2	1	5
Burglary	Male	1592	1421	1433	1279	1267	1286	1087	1070	964	802
	Female	29	19	29	34	32	24	31	39	30	49
Robbery	Male	286	248	189	156	184	177	131	192	163	70
	Female	2	3	11	2	4	2	3	8	1	6
Theft	Male	3171	2971	3036	2981	2860	2967	2839	2907	2628	2408
	Female	745	664	770	810	696	712	659	656	644	589
Fraud and forgery	Male	581	635	586	514	564	569	500	479	430	420
	Female	148	194	154	170	167	146	114	129	132	111
Criminal damage	Male	1104	972	1161	1177	1011	1281	1301	1177	1318	1388
	Female	46	67	51	51	66	96	86	88	96	106
Offences against the state	Male	265	243	287	205	197	187	163	185	183	187
	Female	16	10	23	17	22	19	10	10	7	5
Other offences	Male	400	346	271	346	447	560	648	839	832	629
	Female	26	51	17	18	28	40	46	60	64	41
TOTAL INDICTABLE OFFENCES	Male	9157	8593	9110	8606	8377	8853	8410	8880	8461	7682
	Female	1119	1143	1217	1241	1159	1183	1079	1139	1158	1086
	TOTAL	10276	9736	10327	9847	9536	10036	9489	10019	9619	8768
SUMMARY OFFENCES [1]	Male	6442	5566	4653	4481	4211	4385	4727	4511	4832	4852
	Female	652	599	515	504	546	541	525	505	578	618
	TOTAL	7094	6165	5168	4985	4757	4926	5252	5016	5410	5470
MOTORING OFFENCES [2]	Male	27072	24707	25607	19329	19992	21221	20836	19391	17526	17786
	Female	2783	2613	3004	2063	2165	2270	2090	2233	2256	2447
	TOTAL	29855	27320	28611	21392	22157	23491	22926	21624	19782	20233
TOTAL NUMBER OF PERSONS PROCEEDED AGAINST		47225	43221	44106	36224	36450	38453	37667	36659	34811	34471

Notes:　(1)　Excluding motoring offences.
　　　　(2)　Indictable and Summary motoring offences.

TABLE 4.2: Magistrates' courts: Outcome for principal offence by plea and finding (Adults and Juveniles) 1988-1997

CRIME CATEGORY		1988	1989	1990	1991	1992	1993	1994	1995	1996	1997
INDICTABLE OFFENCES											
Persons proceeded against		10276	9736	10327	9847	9536	10036	9489	10019	9619	8768
Number of findings		9116	8497	9147	8711	8571	9133	8702	9048	8716	8286
PLEA:	not guilty	1205	1036	1323	1321	1502	1603	1539	1654	2049	1702
	guilty	7911	7461	7824	7390	7069	7530	7163	7394	6667	6584
FINDING:	not guilty	895	809	1083	1027	1148	1335	1384	1472	1657	1528
	guilty	8221	7688	8064	7684	7423	7798	7318	7576	7059	6756
% Not guilty pleas		13	12	14	15	18	18	18	18	24	21
% Not guilty findings		10	10	12	12	13	15	16	16	19	18
% Not guilty pleas resulting in not guilty findings		74	78	82	78	76	83	90	89	81	90
SUMMARY OFFENCES											
Persons proceeded against		7094	6165	5168	4985	4757	4926	5252	5016	5410	5470
Number of findings		7094	6165	5168	4985	4756	4926	5252	5016	5405	5468
PLEA:	not guilty	1534	1286	1065	884	953	828	1025	1020	1304	1280
	guilty	5560	4879	4103	4101	3803	4098	4227	3996	4101	4188
FINDING:	not guilty	1023	1052	875	708	642	624	886	879	1017	1042
	guilty	6071	5113	4293	4277	4114	4302	4366	4137	4388	4426
% Not guilty pleas		22	21	21	18	20	17	20	20	24	23
% Not guilty findings		14	17	17	14	14	13	17	18	19	19
% Not guilty pleas resulting in not guilty findings		67	82	82	80	67	75	86	86	78	81
MOTORING OFFENCES											
Persons proceeded against		29855	27320	28611	21392	22157	23491	22926	21624	19782	20233
Number of findings		29847	27307	28590	21368	22146	23477	22919	21605	19770	20227
PLEA:	not guilty	1960	1684	1902	1671	2213	2122	1776	1690	2115	1781
	guilty	27887	25623	26688	19697	19933	21355	21143	19915	17655	18446
FINDING:	not guilty	1294	1211	1383	1235	1359	1615	1445	1503	1622	1484
	guilty	28553	26096	27207	20133	20787	21862	21474	20102	18148	18743
% Not guilty pleas		7	6	7	8	10	9	8	8	11	9
% Not guilty findings		4	4	5	6	6	7	6	7	8	7
% Not guilty pleas resulting in not guilty findings		66	72	73	74	61	76	81	89	77	83

TABLE 4.3: Magistrates' courts: Juveniles proceeded against by principal offence and gender 1988-1997

CRIME CATEGORY		1988	1989	1990	1991	1992	1993	1994	1995	1996	1997
Violence against the person	Male	58	35	39	42	44	32	41	50	78	50
	Female	4	5	8	2	7	14	12	11	15	6
Sexual offences	Male	15	16	18	17	10	11	8	15	13	12
	Female	0	0	0	0	0	0	0	0	0	2
Burglary	Male	263	232	241	201	177	168	197	173	152	136
	Female	4	3	1	3	1	1	7	11	6	6
Robbery	Male	19	15	11	8	4	5	13	26	20	12
	Female	1	0	2	0	0	1	0	1	0	4
Theft	Male	397	299	315	303	232	291	276	332	336	334
	Female	56	31	38	53	35	31	42	43	52	56
Fraud and forgery	Male	7	14	10	10	16	14	14	14	10	11
	Female	0	1	0	3	1	3	2	8	5	0
Criminal damage	Male	126	128	98	107	81	101	138	132	140	154
	Female	3	4	2	2	2	9	8	7	11	13
Offences against the state	Male	19	14	8	5	6	2	10	12	9	12
	Female	2	0	0	0	0	0	0	0	0	0
Other offences	Male	11	9	10	9	9	3	6	15	25	10
	Female	0	2	1	0	0	0	0	0	2	1
TOTAL INDICTABLE OFFENCES	Male	915	762	750	702	579	627	703	769	783	731
	Female	70	46	52	63	46	59	71	81	91	88
	TOTAL	985	808	802	765	625	686	774	850	874	819
SUMMARY OFFENCES [1]	Male	200	201	153	107	117	113	128	189	193	200
	Female	22	24	17	19	11	21	24	24	31	30
	TOTAL	222	225	170	126	128	134	152	213	224	230
MOTORING OFFENCES [2]	Male	108	86	95	66	44	50	78	83	61	63
	Female	2	2	5	6	1	2	3	2	5	2
	TOTAL	110	88	100	72	45	52	81	85	66	65
TOTAL NUMBER OF PERSONS PROCEEDED AGAINST		1317	1121	1072	963	798	872	1007	1148	1164	1114

Notes: (1) Excluding motoring offences.
        (2) Indictable and Summary motoring offences.

TABLE 4.4: Magistrates' courts: Outcome for principal offence by plea and finding for Juveniles 1988-1997

CRIME CATEGORY		1988	1989	1990	1991	1992	1993	1994	1995	1996	1997
INDICTABLE OFFENCES											
Juveniles proceeded against		985	808	802	765	625	686	774	850	874	819
Number of findings		956	771	771	728	605	672	753	822	845	806
PLEA:	not guilty	74	60	60	76	76	104	102	109	144	137
	guilty	882	711	712	652	529	568	651	713	701	669
FINDING:	not guilty	65	54	45	66	51	86	98	98	127	126
	guilty	891	717	726	662	554	586	655	724	718	680
% Not guilty pleas		8	8	8	10	13	15	14	13	17	17
% Not guilty findings		7	7	6	9	8	13	13	12	15	16
% Not guilty pleas resulting in not guilty findings		88	90	76	87	67	83	96	90	88	92
SUMMARY OFFENCES											
Juveniles proceeded against		222	225	170	126	128	134	152	213	224	230
Number of findings		222	225	170	126	128	134	152	213	224	230
PLEA:	not guilty	43	43	36	20	26	12	23	38	61	46
	guilty	179	182	134	106	102	122	129	175	163	184
FINDING:	not guilty	32	39	32	15	15	9	21	33	43	32
	guilty	190	186	138	111	113	125	131	180	181	198
% Not guilty pleas		19	19	21	16	20	9	15	18	27	20
% Not guilty findings		14	17	19	12	12	7	14	15	19	14
% Not guilty pleas resulting in not guilty findings		74	91	89	75	58	75	91	87	70	70
MOTORING OFFENCES											
Juveniles proceeded against		110	88	100	72	45	52	81	85	66	65
Number of findings		110	88	99	72	45	51	81	84	66	65
PLEA:	not guilty	11	8	14	4	6	7	8	10	13	8
	guilty	99	80	85	68	39	44	73	74	53	57
FINDING:	not guilty	10	7	8	1	5	7	8	10	8	8
	guilty	100	81	91	71	40	44	73	74	58	57
% Not guilty pleas		10	9	14	6	13	14	10	12	20	12
% Not guilty findings		9	8	8	1	11	14	10	12	12	12
% Not guilty pleas resulting in not guilty findings		91	88	57	25	83	100	100	100	62	100

TABLE 4.5: The Crown Court: Persons proceeded against by principal offence and gender (Adults and Juveniles) 1988-1997

CRIME CATEGORY		1988	1989	1990	1991	1992	1993	1994	1995	1996	1997
Violence against the person	Male	300	291	394	373	311	404	352	324	273	233
	Female	18	25	23	28	22	24	29	18	10	17
Sexual offences	Male	102	114	129	107	104	75	80	96	110	91
	Female	1	1	0	1	1	1	1	3	0	1
Burglary	Male	181	129	97	133	121	116	91	57	59	58
	Female	0	0	5	4	3	1	3	2	3	1
Robbery	Male	290	280	212	154	210	157	166	180	150	151
	Female	1	5	7	7	4	2	3	7	4	3
Theft	Male	184	134	141	172	169	143	160	151	101	103
	Female	36	28	45	36	32	40	29	21	21	22
Fraud and forgery	Male	69	89	79	58	52	33	41	44	32	48
	Female	13	15	6	10	14	7	7	11	7	7
Criminal damage	Male	135	91	92	64	89	66	73	68	54	71
	Female	2	7	4	4	7	7	5	5	3	3
Offences against the state	Male	41	56	70	66	78	66	41	58	12	16
	Female	3	14	13	10	11	11	2	1	0	0
Other offences (1)	Male	103	83	99	105	69	111	120	184	344	277
	Female	7	5	6	10	7	9	14	19	22	26
TOTALS	Male	1405	1267	1313	1232	1203	1171	1124	1162	1135	1048
	Female	81	100	109	110	101	102	93	87	70	80
	TOTAL	**1486**	**1367**	**1422**	**1342**	**1304**	**1273**	**1217**	**1249**	**1205**	**1128**

Note: (1) Includes Motoring Offences.

TABLE 4.6: The Crown Court: Persons proceeded against by offence group; scheduled and non-scheduled offences (Adults and Juveniles) 1988-1997

OFFENCE GROUP	1988	1989	1990	1991	1992	1993	1994	1995	1996	1997
Scheduled	515	456	470	423	413	447	399	420	170	129
Non-scheduled	971	911	952	919	891	826	818	829	1035	999
TOTAL	**1486**	**1367**	**1422**	**1342**	**1304**	**1273**	**1217**	**1249**	**1205**	**1128**

TABLE 4.7: The Crown Court: Outcome for principal offence by plea and finding (Adults and Juveniles) 1988-1997

		1988	1989	1990	1991	1992	1993	1994	1995	1996	1997
Persons proceeded against		1486	1367	1422	1342	1304	1273	1217	1249	1205	1128
PLEA:	not guilty	261	227	320	282	330	361	283	172	211	141
	guilty	1225	1140	1102	1060	974	912	934	1077	994	987
FINDING:	not guilty	119	133	166	133	169	151	159	92	124	89
	guilty	1367	1234	1256	1209	1135	1122	1058	1157	1081	1039
% Not guilty pleas		18	17	23	21	25	28	23	14	18	13
% Not guilty findings		8	10	12	10	13	12	13	7	10	8
% Not guilty pleas resulting in not guilty findings		46	59	52	47	51	42	56	53	59	63

TABLE 4.8: The Crown Court: Juveniles proceeded against by principal offence and finding 1988-1997

CRIME CATEGORY		1988	1989	1990	1991	1992	1993	1994	1995	1996	1997
Violence against the person		5	4	6	3	6	4	10	2	2	7
Sexual offences		1	3	4	4	2	1	3	0	0	2
Burglary		4	6	0	12	6	5	4	4	5	0
Robbery		7	6	6	5	7	2	2	8	3	5
Theft		4	4	2	4	4	0	4	5	0	5
Fraud and forgery		0	0	0	0	0	0	0	0	1	0
Criminal damage		3	6	9	8	14	2	0	11	0	1
Offences against the state		2	3	0	0	0	0	0	1	0	0
Other offences		0	4	2	2	0	0	1	0	6	2
TOTAL		26	36	29	38	39	14	24	31	17	22
of which:	Male	26	34	28	34	36	14	19	31	13	21
	Female	0	2	1	4	3	0	5	0	4	1
PLEA	not guilty	6	1	8	8	8	4	6	1	2	3
	guilty	20	35	21	30	31	10	18	30	15	19
FINDING	not guilty	5	1	6	7	4	0	4	0	2	2
	guilty	21	35	23	31	35	14	20	31	15	20

TABLE 4.9: Scheduled offences: Persons proceeded against by principal offence and finding (Adults and Juveniles) 1988-1997

CRIME CATEGORY		1988	1989	1990	1991	1992	1993	1994	1995	1996	1997
Violence against the person		156	139	181	179	130	204	134	148	33	42
Burglary		4	7	9	4	10	6	23	2	2	4
Robbery		226	188	143	97	149	116	136	135	67	30
Theft		0	0	0	0	0	0	11	7	5	0
Fraud and forgery		0	0	0	0	0	0	3	1	0	0
Criminal damage		76	53	51	28	28	28	38	26	26	34
Offences against the state		40	59	69	74	80	71	37	45	11	8
Other offences		13	10	17	41	16	22	17	56	26	11
TOTAL		**515**	**456**	**470**	**423**	**413**	**447**	**399**	**420**	**170**	**129**
of which:	Male	503	428	445	390	385	425	385	399	168	127
	Female	12	28	25	33	28	22	14	21	2	2
PLEA	not guilty	73	83	84	80	112	119	80	60	42	18
	guilty	442	373	386	343	301	328	319	360	128	111
FINDING	not guilty	28	42	30	35	59	34	35	23	21	9
	guilty	487	414	440	388	354	413	364	397	149	120

TABLE 4.10: Scheduled offences: Juveniles proceeded against by principal offence and finding 1988-1997

CRIME CATEGORY		1988	1989	1990	1991	1992	1993	1994	1995	1996	1997
Violence against the person		2	1	4	0	0	0	1	0	0	0
Burglary		0	1	0	0	0	1	1	0	0	0
Robbery		4	3	1	4	6	2	2	5	1	0
Theft		0	0	0	0	0	0	0	1	0	0
Criminal damage		3	3	4	2	3	1	0	0	0	0
Offences against the state		2	2	0	0	0	0	0	0	0	0
TOTAL		**11**	**10**	**9**	**6**	**9**	**4**	**4**	**6**	**1**	**0**
of which:	Male	11	9	9	4	9	4	3	6	1	0
	Female	0	1	0	2	0	0	1	0	0	0
PLEA	not guilty	1	0	1	2	1	0	0	1	0	0
	guilty	10	10	8	4	8	4	4	5	1	0
FINDING	not guilty	1	0	1	2	1	0	0	0	0	0
	guilty	10	10	8	4	8	4	4	6	1	0

TABLE 4.11: Persons found guilty (all courts) by age and gender 1997 and rates per 10,000 population

	AGE GROUP	NUMBER OF PERSONS IN AGE GROUP				NUMBER PER 10,000 POPULATION			
		INDICTABLE	SUMMARY	MOTORING	TOTAL	INDICTABLE	SUMMARY	MOTORING	TOTAL
MALE	10-14	181	39	10	230	26	6	1	34
	15-19	1890	913	1897	4700	294	142	295	730
	20-24	1724	1034	3479	6237	270	162	544	975
	25-29	1077	637	2788	4502	167	99	431	696
	30-34	771	496	2183	3450	122	78	344	544
	35-39	505	327	1509	2341	87	56	260	403
	40-44	271	209	1075	1555	52	40	207	300
	45-49	166	134	801	1101	34	28	165	227
	50-54	106	81	554	741	23	18	120	160
	55-59	43	52	337	432	11	14	89	114
	60-64	32	27	171	230	10	8	51	69
	65-69	15	7	92	114	5	2	32	39
	70+	3	6	43	52	1	1	8	9
	Unknown	60	62	1626	1748				
FEMALE	10-14	21	1	6	28	3	0	1	4
	15-19	221	167	87	475	36	27	14	77
	20-24	207	400	70	677	35	68	12	116
	25-29	137	394	74	605	21	62	12	95
	30-34	95	319	61	475	14	48	9	72
	35-39	99	215	41	355	16	35	7	58
	40-44	53	160	23	236	10	31	4	45
	45-49	31	101	20	152	6	21	4	31
	50-54	22	75	14	111	5	16	3	23
	55-59	16	44	5	65	4	11	1	16
	60-64	3	20	2	25	1	5	1	7
	65-69	2	11	1	14	1	3	0	4
	70+	0	8	0	8	0	1	0	1
	Unknown	8	290	7	305				
MALES		6844	16565	4024	27433	100	241	59	400
FEMALES		915	2205	411	3531	13	30	6	48
TOTAL		**7759**	**18770**	**4435**	**30964**	**55**	**133**	**31**	**219**

TABLE 4.12: Percentage of persons found guilty having previous conviction(s) (Adults and Juveniles) 1988-1997

	1988	1989	1990	1991	1992	1993	1994	1995	1996	1997
MALE										
The Crown Court	77	75	76	80	80	79	80	74	68	67
Magistrates' Court - Indictable Offences	65	65	59	73	70	69	69	69	65	62
Magistrates' Court - Summary Offences	62	62	61	70	67	66	67	62	60	53
Magistrates' Court - Motoring Offences	52	54	55	56	55	54	56	56	55	57
FEMALE										
The Crown Court	22	27	50	40	47	41	54	46	44	37
Magistrates' Court - Indictable Offences	36	36	34	46	46	47	51	50	54	49
Magistrates' Court - Summary Offences	36	39	43	46	42	42	45	44	45	25
Magistrates' Court - Motoring Offences	17	19	18	20	21	22	26	26	24	39

5. Sentencing

Introduction

5.1 This chapter deals with persons convicted and sentenced in Northern Ireland courts. Analysis of sentencing is based on the most severe penalty imposed by the court for the principal offence. No account is taken of the outcome of any subsequent appeal.

5.2 When sentencing convicted offenders, Judges and Magistrates can impose a variety of sanctions within the limits prescribed by Parliament. They can choose from a variety of options such as fines or discharges. They can decide on an amount of community supervision required for an offender as in the case of probation or community service orders, or they can consider some form of imprisonment. Appendix 3 summarises the main sentences available to the courts. In imposing sentences, Judges and Magistrates will take account of the characteristics of the offender such as age, previous convictions, financial and domestic circumstances, and characteristics of the offence in terms of seriousness and the degree of culpability.

5.3 Changes in the different types of sentence are not necessarily a reflection of changes in sentencing practice but may be due to variations in any of the factors referred to above. Trends in sentencing over time must therefore be interpreted with caution. A procedural change in the classification of all triable-either-way offences into the indictable category further confounds comparison of 1986 and subsequent data with that for earlier years. This chapter does however provide basic information on the demands made on those agencies which supervise convicted offenders such as prisons and probation. More specifically the chapter identifies and distinguishes the sentences imposed in the magistrates' court and the Crown Court for juveniles and adults. It further identifies in the Crown Court those individuals whose offences were scheduled i.e. listed in relevant schedules of the Northern Ireland (Emergency Provisions) Acts 1978-1996.

Crown Court Sentencing

5.4 In total 1,039 persons were sentenced at the Crown Court during 1997, a decrease of 4% on 1996. Of that total, 590 (57%) were sentenced to immediate custody, the highest proportion since 1993. A further 280 (27%) received a suspended custodial sentence. In 1997 there were 37 community service orders and 47 probation orders representing 8% of all sentences given. Proportionately this rate of supervision in the community (8%) was the lowest proportion recorded during the 1988-1997 period.

5.5 Immediate custodial sentences tend to be given more frequently for scheduled offences than non-scheduled offences, and this continued to be the case in 1997 (see Figure 5.2). Of the 120 persons convicted of scheduled offences in 1997, 68% received immediate custodial sentences. This is the same rate as in 1996. A further 25% received suspended custodial sentences and 8% supervision in the community. This compares with 55% being given immediate custody, 27% receiving suspended custody and 8% receiving supervision in the community for non-scheduled offences in 1997.

Figure 5.1: CROWN COURT SENTENCING BY DISPOSAL 1988-1997

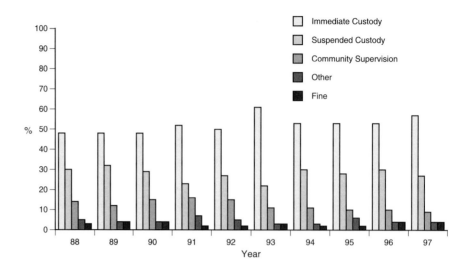

**Figure 5.2: CROWN COURT SENTENCING BY DISPOSAL AND
SCHEDULED STATUS 1997**

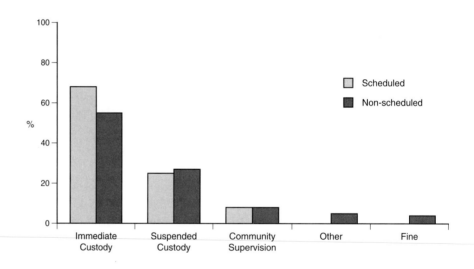

Magistrates' Courts

5.6 In 1997, 29,925 offenders were sentenced at magistrates' courts, of which 6,756 were for indictable offences, 4,426 for summary offences, and 18,743 for motoring offences. The number of motoring offenders, who make up 63% of those sentenced, increased by 3% over the previous year (18,147), while the number convicted for the indictable and summary offences decreased by 2% from 11,446 to 11,182.

5.7 Figures 5.3-5.5 show that for each offence classification the fine was the most common disposal. In 1997 fines were given for 28% of indictable offences, 48% of summary offences, and 92% of motoring offences. In relative terms immediate custodial sentences are less frequently used than in the Crown Court, reflecting the less serious nature of the offences dealt with. In 1997 immediate custodial disposals were given for 17% of indictable offences, 3% of summary offences and 2% of motoring offences. In total 1,567 offenders

34

received sentences of immediate custody from the magistrates' courts in 1997. This figure was nearly three times the number given immediate custody at the Crown Court. Comparing 1997 to 1996 the proportionate use of immediate custody in magistrates' courts was equal at 5% of all disposals. The proportion of fines in 1997 was 71% of all sentences, one percentage point higher than in 1996.

Figure 5.3: MAGISTRATES' COURTS SENTENCING FOR INDICTABLE OFFENCES BY DISPOSAL 1997

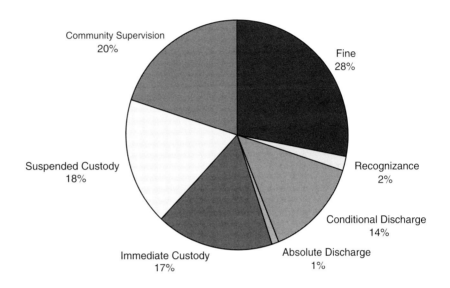

Figure 5.4: MAGISTRATES' COURTS SENTENCING FOR SUMMARY OFFENCES BY DISPOSAL 1997

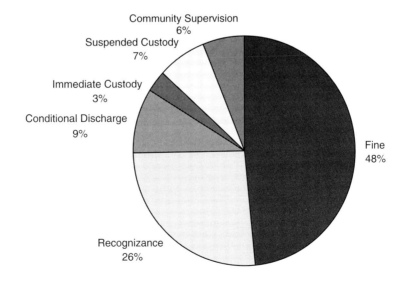

Percentages may not add to 100 due to rounding.

Figure 5.5: MAGISTRATES' COURTS SENTENCING FOR MOTORING OFFENCES BY DISPOSAL 1997

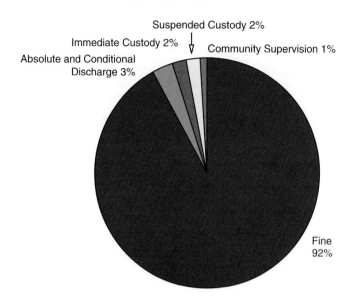

5.8 Figure 5.6 illustrates the annual proportions of the various disposals at magistrates' courts for indictable and summary offences in the last decade. Fines have fallen to 36% of all disposals in 1997 from a peak of 47% in 1989.

Figure 5.6: MAGISTRATES' COURTS SENTENCING FOR INDICTABLE AND SUMMARY OFFENCES BY DISPOSAL 1988-1997

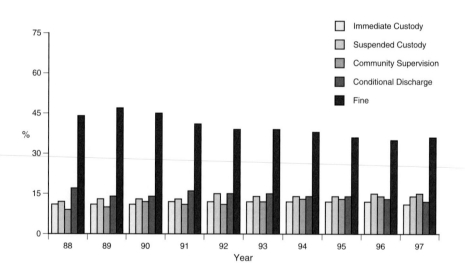

Juvenile Sentences

5.9 In 1997 there were 955 juveniles sentenced by the courts, 700 for indictable offences, 198 for summary offences, and 57 for motoring offences. 180 juveniles were sentenced to immediate custody (most being sent to a training school) in 1997 constituting 19% of all juvenile disposals. This rate shows a decrease of one percentage point from the 1996 rate of 20%. Figure 5.7 shows the relative use of various disposals for juveniles convicted of summary and indictable crime. Only a small number of motoring offences are committed by juveniles (taking and driving away is an offence of theft), so they have been excluded from this chart.

Figure 5.7: ALL COURT JUVENILE SENTENCING FOR INDICTABLE AND SUMMARY OFFENCES BY DISPOSAL 1988-1997

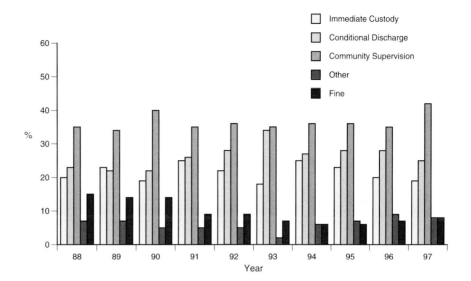

5.10 Disposals given to juveniles for indictable and summary offences by the courts vary from those given to adults, in part reflecting the different nature of offences of which juveniles are found guilty. Figure 5.8 compares the disposals given to juveniles convicted of indictable and summary offences with those given to adults. Juveniles found guilty are more likely to receive custodial supervision (mainly Training School Orders), supervision in the community or a conditional discharge; but less likely to receive a suspended sentence, be released on recognizance or given a fine.

Figure 5.8: ALL COURT DISPOSALS GIVEN TO JUVENILES AND ADULTS[1] CONVICTED OF INDICTABLE AND SUMMARY OFFENCES 1997

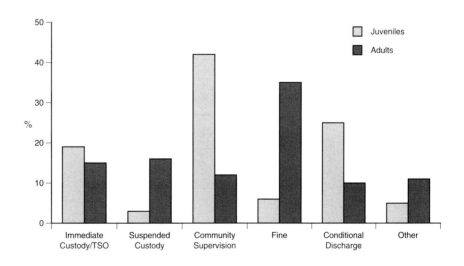

[1] Includes all those aged 17+, missing ages, public bodies and companies

TABLE 5.1: Crown Court sentencing by disposal 1988-1997

SENTENCE — **NUMBER OF PERSONS**

SENTENCE	1988	1989	1990	1991	1992	1993	1994	1995	1996	1997
Prison	536	472	493	493	447	555	471	533	469	475
Young Offenders' Centre	112	111	106	125	119	130	87	76	106	111
Training School	5	10	4	13	5	2	5	6	0	4
Total Immediate Custody	653	593	603	631	571	687	563	615	575	590
Prison Suspended/Recorded	313	318	295	238	249	211	277	265	253	220
YOC Suspended/Recorded	93	73	78	46	63	37	43	63	71	60
Attendance Centre	1	2	0	0	0	0	1	0	0	0
Probation/Supervision	80	72	85	103	95	73	58	60	49	47
Community Service Order	106	71	105	89	79	48	59	60	54	37
Fine	35	39	33	23	17	33	23	27	39	40
Recognizance	7	3	8	7	9	5	16	0	7	10
Conditional Discharge	65	51	37	53	36	19	15	64	30	31
Absolute Discharge	5	1	2	5	8	3	2	1	0	1
Fine plus Disqualification	4	8	10	6	2	0	0	0	0	0
Other	5	3	0	8	6	6	1	2	3	3
All Sentences	1367	1234	1256	1209	1135	1122	1058	1157	1081	1039

PERCENTAGE OF ALL SENTENCES

SENTENCE	1988	1989	1990	1991	1992	1993	1994	1995	1996	1997
Prison	39	38	39	41	40	49	45	46	43	46
Young Offenders' Centre	8	9	8	10	10	12	8	7	10	11
Training School	0	1	0	1	0	0	0	1	0	0
Total Immediate Custody	48	48	48	52	50	61	53	53	53	57
Prison Suspended/Recorded	23	26	23	20	22	19	26	23	23	21
YOC Suspended/Recorded	7	6	6	4	6	3	4	5	7	6
Attendance Centre	0	0	0	0	0	0	0	0	0	0
Probation/Supervision	6	6	7	9	8	7	6	5	5	5
Community Service Order	8	6	8	7	7	4	6	5	5	4
Fine	3	3	3	2	1	3	2	2	4	4
Recognizance	1	0	1	1	1	0	2	0	1	1
Conditional Discharge	5	4	3	4	3	2	1	6	3	3
Absolute Discharge	0	0	0	0	1	0	0	0	0	0
Fine plus Disqualification	0	1	1	0	0	0	0	0	0	0
Other	0	0	0	1	1	1	0	0	0	0

Note: (1)   Percentage components may not add to 100 due to rounding.

TABLE 5.2: Crown Court sentencing for scheduled offences by disposal 1988-1997

SENTENCE   **NUMBER OF PERSONS**

	1988	1989	1990	1991	1992	1993	1994	1995	1996	1997
Prison	221	203	203	225	186	270	217	235	87	69
Young Offenders' Centre	44	34	53	48	36	39	26	26	14	12
Training School	4	1	0	0	1	0	1	1	0	0
Total Immediate Custody	269	238	256	273	223	309	244	262	101	81
Prison Suspended/Recorded	104	85	78	60	74	61	68	72	26	24
YOC Suspended/Recorded	43	37	42	15	30	19	11	25	13	6
Attendance Centre	0	0	0	0	0	0	1	0	0	0
Probation/Supervision	13	17	17	12	12	15	14	15	6	1
Community Service Order	41	21	39	23	8	4	16	11	2	8
Fine	2	0	0	0	0	1	0	0	1	0
Recognizance	2	0	1	1	1	0	8	0	0	0
Conditional Discharge	13	16	7	1	2	4	2	12	0	0
Absolute Discharge	0	0	0	1	4	0	0	0	0	0
Fine plus Disqualification	0	0	0	0	0	0	0	0	0	0
Other	0	0	0	2	0	0	0	0	0	0
All Sentences	487	414	440	388	354	413	364	397	149	120

PERCENTAGE OF ALL SENTENCES

	1988	1989	1990	1991	1992	1993	1994	1995	1996	1997
Prison	45	49	46	58	53	65	60	59	58	58
Young Offenders' Centre	9	8	12	12	10	9	7	7	9	10
Training School	1	0	0	0	0	0	0	0	0	0
Total Immediate Custody	55	57	58	70	63	75	67	66	68	68
Prison Suspended/Recorded	21	21	18	15	21	15	19	18	17	20
YOC Suspended/Recorded	9	9	10	4	8	5	3	6	9	5
Attendance Centre	0	0	0	0	0	0	0	0	0	0
Probation/Supervision	3	4	4	3	3	4	4	4	4	1
Community Service Order	8	5	9	6	2	1	4	3	1	7
Fine	0	0	0	0	0	0	0	0	1	0
Recognizance	0	0	0	0	0	0	2	0	0	0
Conditional Discharge	3	4	2	0	1	1	1	3	0	0
Absolute Discharge	0	0	0	0	1	0	0	0	0	0
Fine plus Disqualification	0	0	0	0	0	0	0	0	0	0
Other	0	0	0	1	0	0	0	0	0	0

Note: (1)   Percentage components may not add to 100 due to rounding.

TABLE 5.3: Magistrates' courts sentencing for indictable offences by disposal 1988-1997

SENTENCE — NUMBER OF PERSONS

	1988	1989	1990	1991	1992	1993	1994	1995	1996	1997
Prison	891	767	747	724	618	764	672	763	696	707
Young Offenders' Centre	338	310	313	430	480	469	405	405	347	319
Training School	152	150	138	156	115	114	165	156	134	134
Total Immediate Custody	1381	1227	1198	1310	1213	1347	1242	1324	1177	1160
Prison Suspended/Recorded	1177	1130	1064	955	980	1036	1017	1103	1058	912
YOC Suspended/Recorded	231	259	247	328	363	328	313	292	318	329
Attendance Centre	125	93	97	80	58	86	81	82	75	55
Probation/Supervision	666	648	727	648	708	718	772	890	883	878
Community Service Order	383	341	472	451	364	407	422	401	426	424
Fine	2528	2504	2704	2271	2267	2389	2180	2176	1958	1884
Recognizance	51	52	63	81	89	87	87	95	101	113
Conditional Discharge	1516	1294	1340	1429	1293	1345	1148	1166	1024	963
Absolute Discharge	94	90	101	76	61	49	48	40	30	34
Fine plus Disqualification	51	42	39	40	20	0	0	0	1	0
Other	18	8	12	15	7	6	8	7	7	4
All Sentences	8221	7688	8064	7684	7423	7798	7318	7576	7058	6756

PERCENTAGE OF ALL SENTENCES

	1988	1989	1990	1991	1992	1993	1994	1995	1996	1997
Prison	11	10	9	9	8	10	9	10	10	10
Young Offenders' Centre	4	4	4	6	6	6	6	5	5	5
Training School	2	2	2	2	2	1	2	2	2	2
Total Immediate Custody	17	16	15	17	16	17	17	17	17	17
Prison Suspended/Recorded	14	15	13	12	13	13	14	15	15	13
YOC Suspended/Recorded	3	3	3	4	5	4	4	4	5	5
Attendance Centre	2	1	1	1	1	1	1	1	1	1
Probation/Supervision	8	8	9	8	10	9	11	12	13	13
Community Service Order	5	4	6	6	5	5	6	5	6	6
Fine	31	33	34	30	31	31	30	29	28	28
Recognizance	1	1	1	1	1	1	1	1	1	2
Conditional Discharge	18	17	17	19	17	17	16	15	15	14
Absolute Discharge	1	1	1	1	1	1	0	1	0	1
Fine plus Disqualification	1	1	0	1	0	0	0	0	0	0
Other	0	0	0	0	0	0	0	0	0	0

Note: (1)   Percentage components may not add to 100 due to rounding.

TABLE 5.4: Magistrates' courts sentencing for summary offences by disposal 1988-1997

SENTENCE

NUMBER OF PERSONS

	1988	1989	1990	1991	1992	1993	1994	1995	1996	1997
Prison	164	125	115	113	81	75	90	70	106	80
Young Offenders' Centre	36	33	27	48	55	38	21	21	39	31
Training School	12	13	9	6	5	8	13	8	8	8
Total Immediate Custody	212	171	151	167	141	121	124	99	153	119
Prison Suspended/Recorded	273	244	234	199	248	249	239	235	327	274
YOC Suspended/Recorded	53	42	47	73	89	60	70	42	73	54
Attendance Centre	12	13	12	6	5	6	5	11	12	9
Probation/Supervision	80	111	98	68	106	118	157	164	154	199
Community Service Order	103	65	72	64	61	67	66	75	86	78
Fine	3771	3498	2803	2692	2274	2352	2302	2040	2009	2124
Recognizance	386	357	334	428	620	769	872	905	1096	1149
Conditional Discharge	964	494	404	472	476	489	458	509	435	399
Absolute Discharge	204	110	123	105	90	70	71	56	41	19
Fine plus Disqualification	1	0	1	0	0	0	0	0	0	0
Other	12	8	14	3	4	1	2	1	2	2
All Sentences	6071	5113	4293	4277	4114	4302	4366	4137	4388	4426

PERCENTAGE OF ALL SENTENCES

	1988	1989	1990	1991	1992	1993	1994	1995	1996	1997
Prison	3	2	3	3	2	2	2	2	2	2
Young Offenders' Centre	1	1	1	1	1	1	1	1	1	1
Training School	0	0	0	0	0	0	0	0	0	0
Total Immediate Custody	3	3	4	4	3	3	3	2	3	3
Prison Suspended/Recorded	4	5	5	5	6	6	5	6	7	6
YOC Suspended/Recorded	1	1	1	2	2	1	2	1	2	1
Attendance Centre	0	0	0	0	0	0	0	0	0	0
Probation/Supervision	1	2	2	2	3	3	4	4	4	4
Community Service Order	2	1	2	1	1	2	2	2	2	2
Fine	62	68	65	63	55	55	53	49	46	48
Recognizance	6	7	8	10	15	18	20	22	25	26
Conditional Discharge	16	10	9	11	12	11	10	12	10	9
Absolute Discharge	3	2	3	2	2	2	2	1	1	0
Fine plus Disqualification	0	0	0	0	0	0	0	0	0	0
Other	0	0	0	0	0	0	0	0	0	0

Note:　(1)　Percentage components may not add to 100 due to rounding.

TABLE 5.5: Magistrates' courts sentencing for indictable and summary offences by disposal 1988-1997

SENTENCE

NUMBER OF PERSONS

	1988	1989	1990	1991	1992	1993	1994	1995	1996	1997
Prison	1055	892	862	837	699	839	762	833	802	787
Young Offenders' Centre	374	343	340	478	535	507	426	426	386	350
Training School	164	163	147	162	120	122	178	164	142	142
Total Immediate Custody	1593	1398	1349	1477	1354	1468	1366	1423	1330	1279
Prison Suspended/Recorded	1450	1374	1298	1154	1228	1285	1256	1338	1385	1186
YOC Suspended/Recorded	284	301	294	401	452	388	383	334	391	383
Attendance Centre	137	106	109	86	63	92	86	93	87	64
Probation/Supervision	746	759	825	716	814	836	929	1054	1037	1077
Community Service Order	486	406	544	515	425	474	488	476	512	502
Fine	6299	6002	5507	4963	4541	4741	4482	4216	3967	4008
Recognizance	437	409	397	509	709	856	959	1000	1197	1262
Conditional Discharge	2480	1788	1744	1901	1769	1834	1606	1675	1459	1362
Absolute Discharge	298	200	224	181	151	119	119	96	71	53
Fine plus Disqualification	52	42	40	40	20	0	0	0	1	0
Other	30	16	26	18	11	7	10	8	9	6
All Sentences	14292	12801	12357	11961	11537	12100	11684	11713	11446	11182

PERCENTAGE OF ALL SENTENCES

	1988	1989	1990	1991	1992	1993	1994	1995	1996	1997
Prison	7	7	7	7	6	7	7	7	7	7
Young Offenders' Centre	3	3	3	4	5	4	4	4	3	3
Training School	1	1	1	1	1	1	1	1	1	1
Total Immediate Custody	11	11	11	12	12	12	12	12	12	11
Prison Suspended/Recorded	10	11	11	10	11	11	11	11	12	11
YOC Suspended/Recorded	2	2	2	3	4	3	3	3	3	3
Attendance Centre	1	1	1	1	1	1	1	1	1	1
Probation/Supervision	5	6	7	6	7	7	8	9	9	10
Community Service Order	3	3	4	4	4	4	4	4	4	4
Fine	44	47	45	41	39	39	38	36	35	36
Recognizance	3	3	3	4	6	7	8	9	10	11
Conditional Discharge	17	14	14	16	15	15	14	14	13	12
Absolute Discharge	2	2	2	2	1	1	1	1	1	0
Fine plus Disqualification	0	0	0	0	0	0	0	0	0	0
Other	0	0	0	0	0	0	0	0	0	0

Note: (1)   Percentage components may not add to 100 due to rounding.

TABLE 5.6: Magistrates' courts sentencing for motoring offences by disposal 1988-1997

SENTENCE — NUMBER OF PERSONS

SENTENCE	1988	1989	1990	1991	1992	1993	1994	1995	1996	1997
Prison	167	114	147	123	131	188	183	213	201	202
Young Offenders' Centre	27	25	30	24	53	68	73	57	57	80
Training School	6	5	6	15	0	3	15	5	5	6
Total Immediate Custody	200	144	183	162	184	259	271	275	263	288
Prison Suspended/Recorded	197	170	215	225	192	244	302	336	337	320
YOC Suspended/Recorded	26	18	16	31	55	59	64	51	53	78
Attendance Centre	2	2	9	4	3	2	3	8	4	2
Probation/Supervision	17	19	29	26	35	45	88	83	97	78
Community Service Order	37	29	31	32	39	62	63	71	79	59
Fine	21720	20304	21137	14606	18877	20425	19908	18510	16645	17305
Recognizance	5	3	2	5	4	2	2	1	6	5
Conditional Discharge	227	234	238	201	196	187	224	253	220	235
Absolute Discharge	1358	1105	1050	664	581	571	542	512	438	371
Fine plus Disqualification	4758	4064	4295	4171	620	6	6	2	4	2
Other	6	4	2	6	1	0	1	0	1	0
All Sentences	28553	26096	27207	20133	20787	21862	21474	20102	18147	18743

PERCENTAGE OF ALL SENTENCES

SENTENCE	1988	1989	1990	1991	1992	1993	1994	1995	1996	1997
Prison	1	0	1	1	1	1	1	1	1	1
Young Offenders' Centre	0	0	0	0	0	0	0	0	0	0
Training School	0	0	0	0	0	0	0	0	0	0
Total Immediate Custody	1	1	1	1	1	1	1	1	1	2
Prison Suspended/Recorded	1	1	1	1	1	1	1	2	2	2
YOC Suspended/Recorded	0	0	0	0	0	0	0	0	0	0
Attendance Centre	0	0	0	0	0	0	0	0	0	0
Probation/Supervision	0	0	0	0	0	0	0	0	1	0
Community Service Order	0	0	0	0	0	0	0	0	0	0
Fine	76	78	78	73	91	93	93	92	92	92
Recognizance	0	0	0	0	0	0	0	0	0	0
Conditional Discharge	1	1	1	1	1	1	1	1	1	1
Absolute Discharge	5	4	4	3	3	3	3	3	2	2
Fine plus Disqualification	17	16	16	21	3	0	0	0	0	0
Other	0	0	0	0	0	0	0	0	0	0

Note: (1)   Percentage components may not add to 100 due to rounding.

TABLE 5.7: All court disposals by gender and offence classification 1997

CRIME CATEGORY	Immediate Custody	Suspended Custody	Supervision in the Community	Fine	Conditional Discharge	Other	TOTAL
MALE							
Violence against the person	252	393	152	477	103	65	1442
Sexual offences	71	22	21	9	5	1	129
Burglary	225	121	188	77	61	5	677
Robbery	107	22	27	1	1	1	159
Theft	411	403	508	513	265	13	2113
Fraud and forgery	51	89	71	125	49	4	389
Criminal damage	211	194	203	195	248	32	1083
Offences against the state	25	34	22	53	17	11	162
Other offences	313	81	28	239	26	3	690
TOTAL INDICTABLE OFFENCES	1666	1359	1220	1689	775	135	6844
SUMMARY (1)	109	318	250	2003	331	1013	4024
MOTORING (2)	300	391	131	15264	192	287	16565
ALL OFFENCES	2075	2068	1601	18956	1298	1435	27433
FEMALE							
Violence against the person	11	31	16	57	23	14	152
Sexual offences	0	0	1	0	0	0	1
Burglary	8	4	11	4	11	0	38
Robbery	4	0	3	0	0	0	7
Theft	25	68	130	128	129	3	483
Fraud and forgery	7	20	34	18	21	2	102
Criminal damage	8	8	17	10	28	9	80
Offences against the state	0	0	1	2	0	0	3
Other offences	8	24	7	7	3	0	49
TOTAL INDICTABLE OFFENCES	71	155	220	226	215	28	915
SUMMARY (1)	10	12	36	124	70	159	411
MOTORING (2)	1	12	9	2047	45	91	2205
ALL OFFENCES	82	179	265	2397	330	278	3531
TOTAL							
Violence against the person	263	424	168	534	126	79	1594
Sexual offences	71	22	22	9	5	1	130
Burglary	233	125	199	81	72	5	715
Robbery	111	22	30	1	1	1	166
Theft	436	471	638	641	394	16	2596
Fraud and forgery	58	109	105	143	70	6	491
Criminal damage	219	202	220	205	276	41	1163
Offences against the state	25	34	23	55	17	11	165
Other offences	321	105	35	246	29	3	739
TOTAL INDICTABLE OFFENCES	1737	1514	1440	1915	990	163	7759
SUMMARY (1)	119	330	286	2127	401	1172	4435
MOTORING (2)	301	403	140	17311	237	378	18770
ALL OFFENCES	2157	2247	1866	21353	1628	1713	30964

Notes: (1)   Excluding Motoring Offence.
        (2)   Indictable and Summary Motoring Offences.

TABLE 5.8: All court disposals (percentages) by offence classification 1997

CRIME CATEGORY	Immediate Custody	Suspended Custody	Supervision in the Community	Fine	Conditional Discharge	Other	TOTAL
Violence against the person	16	27	11	34	8	5	100
Sexual offences	55	17	17	7	4	1	100
Burglary	33	17	28	11	10	1	100
Robbery	67	13	18	1	1	1	100
Theft	17	18	25	25	15	1	100
Fraud and forgery	12	22	21	29	14	1	100
Criminal damage	19	17	19	18	24	4	100
Offences against the state	15	21	14	33	10	7	100
Other offences	43	14	5	33	4	0	100
TOTAL INDICTABLE OFFENCES	22	20	19	25	13	2	100
SUMMARY (1)	3	7	6	48	9	26	100
MOTORING (2)	2	2	1	92	1	2	100
ALL OFFENCES	7	7	6	69	5	6	100

Notes: (1)   Excluding Motoring Offences.
       (2)   Indictable and Summary Motoring Offences.
       (3)   Percentage components may not add to 100 due to rounding.

TABLE 5.9: All court juvenile disposals by offence classification 1997

CRIME CATEGORY	Immediate Custody	Suspended Custody	Supervision in the Community	Fine	Conditional Discharge	Other	TOTAL
Violence against the person	11	6	18	4	9	1	49
Sexual offences	1	0	6	0	1	0	8
Burglary	37	3	57	5	21	1	124
Robbery	10	3	4	0	1	0	18
Theft	64	3	156	16	92	3	334
Fraud and forgery	0	0	7	1	3	0	11
Criminal damage	36	4	57	3	35	1	136
Offences against the state	4	0	3	0	2	1	10
Other offences	0	2	2	1	5	0	10
TOTAL INDICTABLE OFFENCES	163	21	310	30	169	7	700
SUMMARY (1)	10	3	66	27	53	39	198
MOTORING (2)	7	1	12	22	14	1	57
ALL OFFENCES	180	25	388	79	236	47	955

TABLE 5.10: All court disposals (percentages) by offence classification 1997

CRIME CATEGORY	Immediate Custody	Suspended Custody	Supervision in the Community	Fine	Conditional Discharge	Other	TOTAL
Violence against the person	22	12	37	8	18	2	100
Sexual offences	13	0	75	0	13	0	100
Burglary	30	2	46	4	17	1	100
Robbery	56	17	22	0	6	0	100
Theft	19	1	47	5	28	1	100
Fraud and forgery	0	0	64	9	27	0	100
Criminal damage	26	3	42	2	26	1	100
Offences against the state	40	0	30	0	20	10	100
Other offences	0	20	20	10	50	0	100
TOTAL INDICTABLE OFFENCES	23	3	44	4	24	1	100
SUMMARY (1)	5	2	33	14	27	20	100
MOTORING (2)	12	2	21	39	25	2	100
ALL OFFENCES	19	3	41	8	25	5	100

Notes: (1)   Excluding Motoring Offences.
       (2)   Indictable and Summary Motoring Offences.
       (3)   Percentage components may not add to 100 due to rounding.

TABLE 5.11: All court juvenile sentencing for indictable and summary offences by disposal 1988-1997

SENTENCE

NUMBER OF PERSONS

	1988	1989	1990	1991	1992	1993	1994	1995	1996	1997
Prison	2	3	2	0	1	0	0	0	1	0
Young Offenders' Centre	54	44	20	31	30	22	29	54	44	32
Training School	167	170	146	170	123	116	174	165	141	141
Total Immediate Custody	223	217	168	201	154	138	203	219	186	173
Prison Suspended/Recorded	5	4	0	1	0	1	0	2	0	0
YOC Suspended/Recorded	22	38	25	19	11	14	17	25	25	24
Attendance Centre	134	99	102	80	61	83	80	92	79	61
Probation/Supervision	248	209	220	172	168	163	183	219	223	293
Community Service Order	1	7	32	26	22	19	23	27	21	22
Fine	166	134	115	67	62	33	49	55	68	57
Recognizance	20	10	8	12	10	26	23	29	42	42
Conditional Discharge	255	206	198	211	199	244	218	262	252	222
Absolute Discharge	14	10	9	8	9	4	9	5	13	4
Fine plus Disqualification	6	3	5	2	2	0	0	0	0	0
Other	8	1	4	5	4	0	0	0	4	0
All Sentences	1102	938	886	804	702	725	805	935	913	898

PERCENTAGE OF ALL SENTENCES

	1988	1989	1990	1991	1992	1993	1994	1995	1996	1997
Prison	0	0	0	0	0	0	0	0	0	0
Young Offenders' Centre	5	5	2	4	4	3	4	6	5	4
Training School	15	18	16	21	18	16	21	18	15	16
Total Immediate Custody	20	23	19	25	22	19	25	23	20	19
Prison Suspended/Recorded	0	0	0	0	0	0	0	0	0	0
YOC Suspended/Recorded	2	4	3	2	2	2	2	3	3	3
Attendance Centre	12	11	12	10	9	11	10	10	9	7
Probation/Supervision	23	22	25	21	24	22	23	23	24	33
Community Service Order	0	1	4	3	3	3	3	3	2	2
Fine	15	14	13	8	9	5	6	6	7	6
Recognizance	2	1	1	1	1	4	3	3	5	5
Conditional Discharge	23	22	22	26	28	34	27	28	28	25
Absolute Discharge	1	1	1	1	1	1	1	1	1	0
Fine plus Disqualification	1	0	1	0	0	0	0	0	0	0
Other	1	0	0	1	1	0	0	0	0	0

Notes: (1) Excluding Motoring Offences.

(2) Percentage components may not add to 100 due to rounding.

6. Prison population

Introduction

6.1 Offenders given an immediate custodial sentence by the Court may be specifically directed to a training school (if under 17), a Young Offenders' Centre (if under 21 and receiving a sentence of up to 4 years) or may be given a more general order of imprisonment or detention. Training schools are not prison service establishments and persons detained there are not included in this chapter. Some information on the use of training schools is included in Chapter 5 and Appendix 3. This chapter therefore provides information on the population of the establishments operated by the Northern Ireland Prison Service to hold persons in legal custody as directed by the courts.

Types of Prisoner

6.2 The prison population consists mainly of offenders sentenced by the courts to immediate custody for criminal offences. It also includes fine defaulters, remand prisoners and a small number of non-criminal or civil prisoners. Immediate custody prisoners and fine defaulters are collectively referred to as sentenced prisoners.

6.3 Fine defaulters are those who have been given a fine by the courts (strictly a fine or custodial sentence), have not paid the fine within a stipulated time, and have then been the subject of a warrant issued by the court. They are a particular type of sentenced criminal prisoner. The duration of sentence is dependent upon the amount of the unpaid fine. This ranges in magistrates' courts from one week where the default is £200 or less, to one year, where it is over £10,000. In the Crown Court the duration of sentence may be up to 10 years where the default is £1 million or more. Fine defaulters aged under 17 are detained in a training school, and are therefore excluded from the statistics in this chapter.

6.4 Remand prisoners include those charged with an offence whom the courts have ruled should be detained in custody pending trial; those whom the courts have permitted to be released on bail pending trial but have not as yet met the conditions (usually financial) of the bail; those who had been released on bail but have subsequently been re-admitted to prison because they breached a condition of bail; and those who have been found guilty by the court but have been ordered to be detained in custody pending sentence. Persons aged under 17 on remand will normally be detained in a training school, and therefore may be excluded from the statistics in this chapter.

6.5 Non-criminal prisoners include those who have been imprisoned for non-payment of maintenance, non-payment of a debt, contempt of court, or are being held under the terms of an Immigration Act.

Counting Rules

6.6 The prison population fluctuates throughout the year and within each week. This is a consequence of factors such as the pattern of court sitting and discharge rules relating to weekends. To remove within-week variation and provide a more consistent approach, prison population statistics are based on counts taken on the last Thursday night of each month. Annual averages are derived from twelve such monthly counts. Annual prison receptions are calculated simply as the sum total of admissions into prisons during the year.

6.7 In general the counting rules in operation closely follow those used by the Home office. Important features of these are:-

- where a person is received more than once a year he will be counted separately on each occasion, including each occasion of change of status between remand and sentenced/fine defaulter;

- where a person is received under sentence for two or more offences, only the principal criminal offence is recorded;

- where a person is received under sentence for two or more offences, sentence length is taken as the longest of any concurrent sentences, with consecutive sentences being treated as one sentence equal in length to the sentences added together; and

- the age of a prisoner is calculated as age at reception.

The Average Prison Population

6.8 The average prison population in Northern Ireland declined steadily between 1988 and 1990. This was followed by 3 consecutive annual increases between 1991 and 1993 (Figure 6.1). In 1997 the average prison population fell for the fourth consecutive year to 1,632 - a very slight decrease compared to 1996 and a fall of 14% compared to 1988.

Figure 6.1: AVERAGE PRISON POPULATION 1969-1997

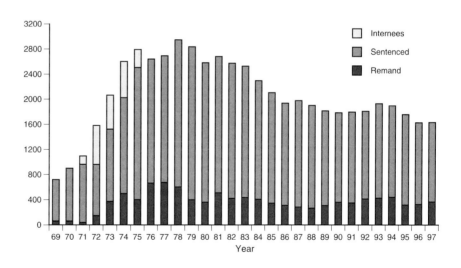

The Average Prison Population by Type of Prisoner

6.9 A comparison of the 1997 and 1996 average prison populations shows that the number of males and females is basically unchanged - an average of 1,610 males in 1996 compared to 1,602 in 1997 and an average of 29 females in 1996 compared to 30 in 1997. Overall prisoners sentenced to immediate custody have fallen by 4% from 1,278 in 1996 to 1,226 in 1997. Fine default prisoners have increased from an average of 24 in 1996 to 30 in 1997 and remand prisoners have increased by 12% from an average of 326 in 1996 to 366 in 1997.

6.10 The last decade has seen a gradual decrease in the average number of those under sentence of immediate custody. The 1997 figure (1,226) is 23% less than that for 1988 (1,593). The average number of remand prisoners peaked at 439 in 1994 before falling in 1995 but has increased in the last two years. The 1997 figure (366) is 17% less than the 1994 peak but is 38% higher than the figure for 1988 (266). During this decade the average number of fine defaulters ranged between 38 in 1998 to 24 in 1996. The 1997 figure was 30. The average number of non-criminal prisoners was very low (1) for the years between 1990 and 1994 however this average increased to 5 in 1995, 11 in 1996 and fell to 10 in 1997.

Figure 6.2: AVERAGE PRISON POPULATION UNDER SENTENCE OF IMMEDIATE CUSTODY BY AGE AND GENDER 1988-1997

Females
Males <21 yrs
Males >=21 yrs
1600
1400
1200
1000
800
600
400
200
0
88
89
90
91
92
93
94
95
96
97
Year

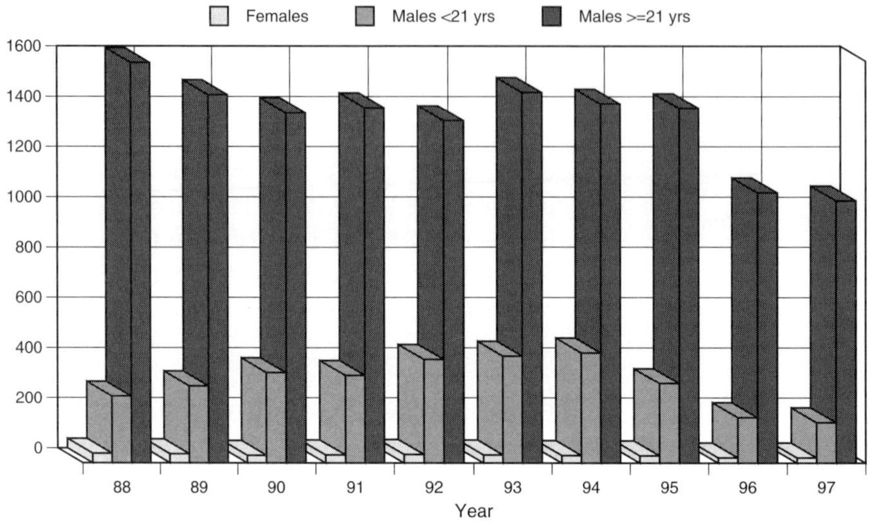

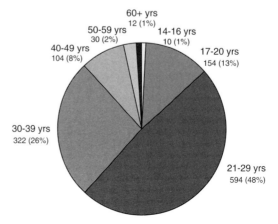

The Average Prison Population by Age

6.11 The age profile of the average prison population is markedly different from the overall Northern Ireland population. In 1997 61% of the average prison population who had been sentenced to immediate custody were between the ages of 17 and 29, with 48% being between the ages of 21 and 29 (Figure 6.3). The equivalent proportions for the population as a whole are 19% (17-29) and 14% (21-29). In the last decade there has been a general downward trend in the average number of immediate custody prisoners aged under 21. The 1997 average (164) is 36% less than 1993 (258) and 57% less than 1988 (383).

Figure 6.3: AVERAGE PRISON POPULATION UNDER SENTENCE OF IMMEDIATE CUSTODY BY AGE 1997

60+ yrs
12 (1%)
50-59 yrs
30 (2%)
14-16 yrs
10 (1%)
40-49 yrs
104 (8%)
17-20 yrs
154 (13%)
30-39 yrs
322 (26%)
21-29 yrs
594 (48%)

Percentages may not add to 100 due to rounding.

6.12 In 1997, 52% of the average immediate custody prison population had committed offences of violence against the person, 13% offences of dishonesty (theft, fraud & forgery, and burglary), 10% offences of robbery, 9% sexual offences, 8% drug offences, and 3% criminal damage offences (Figure 6.4). The average number of sexual offenders in the immediate custody prison population rose from 101 in 1995 to 104 in 1996 then to 113 in 1997. Sexual offenders in 1997 account for 9% of the average immediate custody population compared to 6% in 1988.

Figure 6.4: AVERAGE PRISON POPULATION UNDER SENTENCE OF IMMEDIATE CUSTODY BY OFFENCE 1988-1997

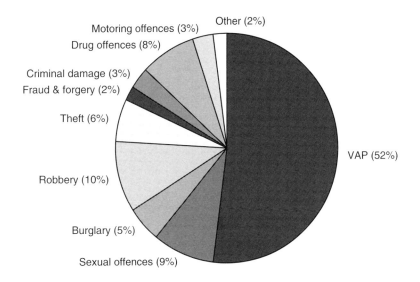

6.13 The number of receptions into prison in Northern Ireland increased for the third consecutive year in 1997. The 1997 figure (5,502) being slightly higher than that for 1996 (5,498) and 12% higher than the 1994 figure (4,897). The 1997 figure is the highest number of receptions recorded in the last decade. Males make up 96% (5,286) of all receptions compared to females (4% - 216). Despite recent increases the total number of receptions (5,502) in 1997 is similar to that of 1988 (5,426) - 1% higher.

6.14 Those received into prison under sentence of immediate custody fell for the second consecutive year. The 1997 figure (1,393) is 3% less than that for 1995 (1,441). The 1997 figure is 11% less than that for 1988 (1,573) although the 1997 figure is not the lowest number of receptions recorded in the last decade - this occurred in 1992 (1,312).

6.15 The number of remand receptions in 1997 (2,188) fell compared to 1996 (2,292) but the number of remand receptions in the last five years has shown a steady increase compared to earlier in the decade. The 1997 figure is 18% higher than that for 1988 (1,853) and 10% higher than the figure for 1992 (1,987).

6.16 Despite constituting a small part of the average prison population (2% in 1997) a substantial number of persons are admitted to prison each year because of fine default. The number of fine defaulters received into prison in 1997 was 1,879. While this represents an increase of 8% on the previous year, it is actually 4% less than the total for 1988 (1,950). Fine defaulters as a percentage of total receptions increased to 34% in 1997, similar to the proportions in 1996 (32%) and 1995 (31%).

Figure 6.5: PRISON RECEPTIONS BY TYPE 1988-1997

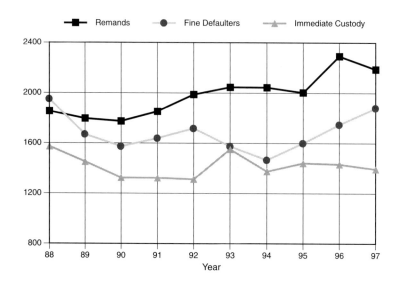

6.17 Non-criminal prisoners comprise only a small part of both the average prison population and prison receptions. As regards receptions of these prisoners, the number rose from 27 in 1996 to 42 in 1997. In the last decade the average number of non-criminal receptions peaked in 1988 (50) and was at its lowest in 1992 (10).

6.18 Remand prisoners (2,188) made up 40% of all receptions in 1997; fine defaulters accounted for 34% (1,879); immediate custody 25% (1,393) and non-criminal prisoners 1% (42). During the last 9 years there has been a consistent trend of remand receptions accounting for most receptions, followed by fine defaulters and then immediate custody receptions - this has been true for each year in the 1989-1997 period.

Comparisons between Prison Receptions and the Prison Population

6.19 Short sentence prisoners account for the greater proportion of immediate custody receptions into prison. However, given their turnover, most of the sentenced prison population at any time are in custody for lengthy sentences. On average in 1997, 15% of those in prison who had been sentenced to immediate custody, had sentences of up to 1 year, 30% had sentences of between 1 and 5 years, 36% had determinate sentences of over 5 years, and 19% were serving life sentences (including those detained at the Secretary of State's pleasure). By contrast, immediate custody receptions into prison show a different pattern. In 1997, 61% of those sentenced to immediate custody were given sentences of 1 year or less, 32% received sentences between 1 and 5 years, 6% had determinate sentences of over 5 years, and only 1% received life sentences (Figures 6.6 and 6.7).

52

Figure 6.6: AVERAGE PRISON POPULATION UNDER SENTENCE OF IMMEDIATE CUSTODY BY SENTENCE LENGTH 1997

Figure 6.7: RECEPTIONS UNDER SENTENCE OF IMMEDIATE CUSTODY BY SENTENCE LENGTH 1997

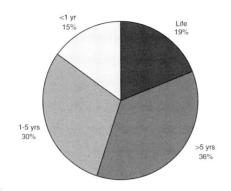

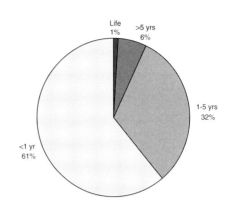

Imprisonment in Northern Ireland and Other Countries

6.20 International comparisons of prison populations are difficult to interpret. A comparison by the Council of Europe indicates that, on the given survey date (1 September 1996) Northern Ireland had a rate of 99 prisoners per 100,000 population of the European jurisdictions surveyed. The comparisons between the prison population and the local demographic population of the country show that England and Wales and Scotland and Northern Ireland were near the top for Western European countries. The rates in Russia (710) and the USA (610) (not shown in the chart) were far higher than any other country.

Figure 6.8: PRISONERS PER 100,000 POPULATION FOR SELECTED JURISDICTIONS 1996

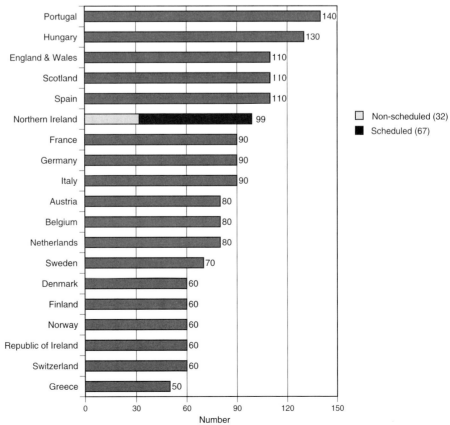

53

TABLE 6.1: Average population in prison establishments, by type of prisoner 1988-1997

	1988	1989	1990	1991	1992	1993	1994	1995	1996	1997
Male Prisoners										
Remand										
Aged under 21	70	82	87	79	93	96	106	72	69	70
Aged 21 or over	188	217	259	254	307	322	321	240	249	288
	258	299	346	333	400	418	427	312	318	358
Fine defaulter										
Aged under 21	8	7	6	8	6	7	4	5	5	6
Aged 21 or over	29	28	23	23	27	23	23	23	19	23
	37	35	29	31	33	30	27	28	24	29
Immediate Custody										
YOC	170	156	134	141	145	153	133	118	115	104
Young Prisoners	210	165	140	116	102	100	91	87	66	57
Adult Prisoners	1193	1129	1105	1136	1088	1192	1179	1177	1076	1044
	1573	1450	1379	1393	1335	1445	1403	1382	1257	1205
Non-Criminal	4	6	1	1	1	1	1	5	11	10
All Males	1872	1790	1755	1758	1769	1894	1858	1727	1610	1602
Female Prisoners										
Remand										
Aged under 21	1	2	6	6	6	2	5	2	2	3
Aged 21 or over	7	6	8	10	7	6	7	3	6	5
	8	8	14	16	13	8	12	5	8	8
Fine defaulter										
Aged under 21	0	0	0	0	0	1	1	0	0	0
Aged 21 or over	1	1	1	1	1	1	2	1	0	1
	1	1	1	1	1	2	3	1	0	1
Immediate Custody										
YOC	1	3	2	2	4	3	4	6	4	3
Young Prisoners	2	1	1	1	2	3	3	2	1	0
Adult Prisoners	17	12	12	18	21	24	19	21	16	18
	20	16	15	21	27	30	26	29	21	21
Non-Criminal	0	0	0	0	0	0	0	0	0	0
All Females	29	25	30	38	41	40	41	35	29	30
All Prisoners										
Remand	266	307	360	349	413	426	439	317	326	366
Fine Defaulter	38	36	30	32	34	32	30	29	24	30
Immediate Custody	1593	1466	1394	1414	1362	1475	1429	1411	1278	1226
Non-Criminal	4	6	1	1	1	1	1	5	11	10
TOTAL	1901	1815	1785	1796	1810	1934	1899	1762	1639	1632

TABLE 6.2: Average prison population under sentence of immediate custody, by duration of sentence given 1988-1997

	1988	1989	1990	1991	1992	1993	1994	1995	1996	1997
Adult Males										
Life	340	337	315	309	270	262	225	232	223	209
>10 years, less than life	169	169	184	209	207	252	282	278	264	246
>5 and <=10 years	177	204	226	242	220	226	244	241	180	157
>4 and <=5 years	83	73	68	67	70	83	88	76	48	45
>3 and <=4 years	80	69	57	58	61	73	62	65	56	62
>2 and <=3 years	100	68	61	57	67	76	67	72	71	92
>1 and <=2 years	94	75	74	77	70	83	86	87	93	102
>6 and <=12 months	84	69	67	60	68	79	72	66	82	78
>3 and <=6 months	53	51	43	46	41	46	40	50	45	42
<=3 months	15	13	10	12	16	12	12	10	14	10
TOTAL	1193	1129	1105	1136	1088	1192	1179	1177	1076	1044
Young Males										
Life	98	86	62	45	35	26	18	17	19	18
>10 years, less than life	36	27	29	26	23	27	29	27	26	25
>5 and <=10 years	40	35	36	35	37	41	37	35	18	12
>4 and <=5 years	24	17	13	9	7	7	7	7	3	2
>3 and <=4 years	13	9	18	23	28	29	23	19	14	14
>2 and <=3 years	57	35	28	36	29	23	26	16	19	23
>1 and <=2 years	39	41	31	30	31	38	28	23	26	21
>6 and <=12 months	43	38	32	28	25	35	36	33	31	23
>3 and <=6 months	26	26	19	21	26	24	18	22	20	18
<=3 months	6	6	6	3	5	5	3	5	5	5
TOTAL	380	321	274	257	247	253	224	205	181	161
Adult Females										
Life	6	6	6	4	3	4	5	6	6	6
>5 years, less than life	3	1	2	5	7	9	8	9	7	6
>1 and <=5 years	5	1	3	7	10	8	3	2	2	1
>6 and <=12 months	1	2	1	0	1	3	0	4	1	2
>3 and <=6 months	1	2	1	1	1	1	2	1	1	3
<=3 months	1	1	0	1	0	1	1	1	1	0
TOTAL	17	12	13	18	21	24	19	21	16	18
Young Females										
Life	0	0	0	0	0	0	0	0	0	0
>5 years, less than life	1	1	1	1	2	3	3	2	1	0
>1 and <=5 years	1	2	1	1	3	2	1	3	1	2
>6 and <=12 months	0	0	0	1	1	0	1	2	1	1
>3 and <=6 months	0	0	0	0	0	1	1	1	1	1
<=3 months	0	0	0	0	0	0	1	0	1	0
TOTAL	3	4	2	3	6	6	7	8	5	3

Notes: (1) Components may not sum to totals due to rounding.
(2) Life includes those detained at the Secretary of State's Pleasure.

TABLE 6.3: Average prison population under sentence of immediate custody, by age at reception 1988-1997

	1988	1989	1990	1991	1992	1993	1994	1995	1996	1997
Male Prisoners										
14-16 years	14	12	12	8	11	13	8	12	9	10
17-20 years	367	308	262	248	234	239	215	193	172	150
21-29 years	832	760	722	713	669	719	707	686	622	584
30-39 years	260	266	278	301	298	331	341	357	324	317
40-49 years	79	81	77	90	90	97	87	91	92	101
50-59 years	17	14	19	24	26	34	34	31	25	30
60+ years	6	8	8	9	5	10	11	11	13	12
TOTAL	1573	1450	1379	1393	1335	1445	1403	1382	1257	1205
Female Prisoners										
14-16 years	0	0	1	0	1	1	1	1	0	0
17-20 years	2	3	2	3	5	5	5	7	4	3
21-29 years	12	9	8	10	15	13	9	11	9	10
30-39 years	2	1	2	6	5	8	6	5	5	5
40-49 years	3	2	3	2	2	3	3	5	2	2
50-59 years	1	1	0	0	0	0	0	0	0	1
60+ years	0	0	0	0	0	0	0	0	0	0
TOTAL	20	16	15	21	27	30	26	29	21	21
All Prisoners										
14-16 years	14	12	13	9	12	14	10	12	9	10
17-20 years	369	311	264	251	239	244	220	200	176	154
21-29 years	844	769	730	722	684	732	717	697	631	594
30-39 years	262	267	280	307	303	339	347	362	329	322
40-49 years	82	83	80	92	91	100	90	97	94	104
50-59 years	18	15	19	24	26	34	34	31	25	30
60+ years	6	8	8	9	5	10	11	11	13	12
TOTAL	1593	1466	1394	1414	1362	1475	1429	1411	1278	1226

Note: (1)   Components may not sum to totals due to rounding.

TABLE 6.4: Average prison population under sentence of immediate custody, by offence 1988-1997

	1988	1989	1990	1991	1992	1993	1994	1995	1996	1997
Adult Males										
Violence against the person	638	628	621	642	596	666	690	694	627	561
Sexual offences	82	89	103	107	110	102	96	92	92	102
Burglary	120	88	69	58	64	74	62	65	43	46
Robbery	161	166	170	151	141	151	146	126	103	96
Theft	81	63	41	57	54	57	50	48	54	54
Fraud & forgery	29	24	28	33	25	33	23	25	24	19
Criminal damage	32	20	18	24	24	27	19	19	16	26
Drug offences	8	9	5	4	6	11	26	37	68	81
Motoring offences	36	20	29	23	23	28	28	30	25	33
Other offences	39	22	22	38	45	44	40	42	24	25
TOTAL	1193	1129	1105	1136	1088	1192	1179	1177	1076	1044
Young Males										
Violence against the person	198	165	135	121	105	95	84	82	68	70
Sexual offences	16	12	21	24	19	16	14	9	11	10
Burglary	65	50	32	33	34	33	29	32	21	17
Robbery	32	33	30	28	41	37	40	31	22	18
Theft	23	23	14	19	16	12	11	12	24	17
Fraud & forgery	3	3	1	2	1	2	1	0	1	1
Criminal damage	27	17	22	15	12	23	13	9	10	6
Drug offences	0	1	0	0	0	6	5	6	14	11
Motoring offences	15	12	13	9	15	22	20	18	4	5
Other offences	10	5	6	5	4	7	7	7	6	5
TOTAL	380	321	274	257	247	253	224	205	181	161
Adult Females										
Violence against the person	13	8	9	13	16	18	14	14	11	10
Sexual offences	1	0	0	0	0	0	0	0	1	1
Burglary	0	0	0	0	0	0	0	0	0	1
Robbery	0	0	1	1	0	1	1	2	1	2
Theft	2	3	1	1	2	2	1	4	3	3
Fraud & forgery	1	1	1	2	1	1	1	1	0	0
Criminal damage	0	0	0	0	1	0	0	1	0	0
Drug offences	0	0	0	0	0	2	1	0	0	0
Motoring offences	0	0	0	0	0	0	0	1	0	0
Other offences	1	0	1	2	1	0	0	0	0	0
TOTAL	17	12	12	18	21	24	19	21	16	18
Young Females										
Violence against the person	2	3	1	2	4	6	3	3	2	1
Sexual offences	0	0	0	0	0	0	0	0	0	0
Burglary	0	0	0	0	0	0	0	0	0	1
Robbery	0	0	0	1	1	0	0	1	0	1
Theft	1	0	0	0	1	0	1	1	0	0
Fraud & forgery	0	0	0	0	0	0	0	1	0	0
Criminal damage	0	0	0	0	0	0	0	0	0	0
Drug offences	0	0	0	0	0	0	0	0	1	0
Motoring offences	0	0	0	0	0	0	0	0	0	0
Other offences	1	0	1	0	1	0	1	2	0	0
TOTAL	3	4	3	3	6	6	7	8	5	3

Note: (1)   Components may not sum to totals due to rounding.

TABLE 6.5: Average prison population under sentence of immediate custody, scheduled and non-scheduled offences 1988-1997

	1988	1989	1990	1991	1992	1993	1994	1995	1996	1997
Scheduled Offences										
Adult Male	848	832	829	849	802	883	887	872	763	703
Young Male	264	223	193	172	161	159	142	124	101	93
Adult Female	14	8	11	15	18	19	15	15	12	12
Young Female	2	3	2	2	5	5	4	5	2	2
TOTAL	1128	1066	1035	1038	986	1066	1048	1016	878	810
Non-Scheduled Offences										
Adult Male	378	297	276	287	287	309	293	305	313	341
Young Male	126	98	81	85	86	94	81	81	79	68
Adult Female	4	4	2	3	3	5	4	6	4	5
Young Female	2	0	0	1	1	0	3	3	2	1
TOTAL	510	399	359	376	377	408	381	395	398	415
OVERALL TOTAL	1638	1466	1394	1414	1362	1475	1429	1411	1278	1226

Notes: (1)   Components may not sum to totals due to rounding.
       (2)   From 1989 the scheduled/non-scheduled categories include only persons sentenced to immediate custody by the courts; figures prior to 1989 included others, such as fine defaulters and non-criminal prisoners.

TABLE 6.6: Receptions into prison establishments, by type of prisoner 1988-1997

	1988	1989	1990	1991	1992	1993	1994	1995	1996	1997
Male Prisoners										
Remand										
Aged under 21	589	623	528	500	596	641	579	627	623	609
Aged 21 or over	1182	1085	1165	1257	1301	1333	1362	1306	1565	1492
	1771	1708	1693	1757	1897	1974	1941	1933	2188	2101
Fine defaulter										
Aged under 21	447	371	296	344	357	335	267	343	362	353
Aged 21 or over	1441	1248	1226	1248	1314	1188	1141	1216	1320	1436
	1888	1619	1522	1592	1671	1523	1408	1559	1682	1789
Immediate Custody										
YOC	430	415	365	339	363	407	332	356	343	321
Young Prisoners	25	30	24	18	15	23	14	14	6	8
Adult Prisoners	1085	974	914	932	903	1086	991	1022	1045	1029
	1540	1419	1303	1289	1281	1516	1337	1392	1394	1358
Non-Criminal	50	46	21	17	10	20	13	45	27	38
All Males	5249	4792	4539	4655	4859	5033	4699	4929	5291	5286
Female Prisoners										
Remand										
Aged under 21	18	30	30	28	28	21	47	23	37	36
Aged 21 or over	64	57	50	66	62	50	55	47	67	51
	82	87	80	94	90	71	102	70	104	87
Fine defaulter										
Aged under 21	10	7	13	12	7	18	9	8	11	13
Aged 21 or over	52	43	38	34	38	33	49	32	54	77
	62	50	51	46	45	51	58	40	65	90
Immediate Custody										
YOC	7	7	6	9	8	9	14	15	19	10
Young Prisoners	1	0	0	2	0	1	0	0	0	0
Adult Prisoners	25	25	15	22	23	25	24	34	19	25
	33	32	21	33	31	35	38	49	38	35
Non-Criminal	0	0	0	0	0	1	0	0	0	4
All Females	177	169	152	173	166	158	198	159	207	216
All Prisoners										
Remand	1853	1795	1773	1851	1987	2045	2043	2003	2292	2188
Fine Defaulter	1950	1669	1573	1638	1716	1574	1466	1599	1747	1879
Immediate Custody	1573	1451	1324	1322	1312	1551	1375	1441	1432	1393
Non-Criminal	50	46	21	17	10	21	13	45	27	42
TOTAL	5426	4961	4691	4828	5025	5191	4897	5088	5498	5502

Note: (1)   Figures shown for the YOC relate to sentences to the YOC establishment. For administrative reasons, the male figures may not equate precisely with the number of persons placed in YOC Hydebank.

TABLE 6.7: Receptions under sentence of immediate custody, by duration of sentence given 1988-1997

	1988	1989	1990	1991	1992	1993	1994	1995	1996	1997
Adult Males										
Life	14	16	16	16	16	19	23	23	11	6
>10 years, less than life	37	32	40	45	32	78	32	51	14	32
>5 and <=10 years	83	74	74	84	55	74	75	68	45	46
>4 and <=5 years	35	37	33	40	33	40	35	32	22	33
>3 and <=4 years	36	35	29	37	33	52	43	53	41	50
>2 and <=3 years	59	56	47	56	63	69	50	83	83	100
>1 and <=2 years	119	103	110	115	107	139	145	134	165	181
>6 and <=12 months	232	182	189	172	184	227	207	189	247	220
>3 and <=6 months	265	265	226	219	212	247	223	254	247	222
<=3 months	205	174	150	148	168	141	158	135	170	139
TOTAL	1085	974	914	932	903	1086	991	1022	1045	1029
Young Males										
Life	4	3	1	1	1	0	0	3	1	1
>10 years, less than life	1	5	3	5	1	10	3	2	2	1
>5 and <=10 years	11	12	16	9	10	8	7	7	2	4
>4 and <=5 years	5	10	4	3	3	5	4	2	1	2
>3 and <=4 years	4	11	12	17	11	22	14	12	7	16
>2 and <=3 years	36	20	28	29	17	25	21	15	23	18
>1 and <=2 years	54	56	44	45	47	51	44	43	48	44
>6 and <=12 months	119	108	97	94	79	112	102	98	101	65
>3 and <=6 months	145	137	114	104	134	139	103	124	103	115
<=3 months	76	83	70	50	75	58	48	64	61	63
TOTAL	455	445	389	357	378	430	346	370	349	329
Adult Females										
Life	0	0	0	0	0	1	2	0	0	0
>5 years, less than life	0	1	1	2	4	1	1	2	0	0
>1 and <=5 years	2	2	7	4	9	4	1	3	6	2
>6 and <=12 months	4	7	2	0	2	7	1	9	2	4
>3 and <=6 months	6	9	2	8	4	3	12	6	3	14
<=3 months	13	6	3	8	4	9	7	14	8	5
TOTAL	25	25	15	22	23	25	24	34	19	25
Young Females										
Life	0	0	0	0	0	0	0	0	0	0
>5 years, less than life	0	0	0	2	0	1	0	0	0	0
>1 and <=5 years	2	2	2	2	3	0	3	2	1	1
>6 and <=12 months	1	0	1	0	2	0	2	6	3	2
>3 and <=6 months	2	3	0	2	2	3	4	2	4	5
<=3 months	3	2	3	5	1	6	5	5	11	2
TOTAL	8	7	6	11	8	10	14	15	19	10

Note: (1) Life includes those detained at the Secretary of State's Pleasure.

TABLE 6.8: Receptions under sentence of immediate custody, by age at reception 1988-1997

	1988	1989	1990	1991	1992	1993	1994	1995	1996	1997
Male Prisoners										
14-16 years	35	41	23	20	25	16	23	49	39	23
17-20 years	420	404	366	337	353	414	323	321	310	306
21-29 years	698	615	611	586	581	682	608	587	599	577
30-39 years	264	248	212	234	204	270	278	296	289	297
40-49 years	87	80	62	82	74	90	72	89	114	111
50-59 years	29	26	22	22	33	29	21	39	31	34
60+ years	7	5	7	8	11	15	12	11	12	10
TOTAL	1540	1419	1303	1289	1281	1516	1337	1392	1394	1358
Female Prisoners										
14-16 years	3	0	1	1	1	0	3	0	3	0
17-20 years	5	7	5	10	7	10	11	15	16	10
21-29 years	11	15	11	12	20	14	12	14	10	13
30-39 years	10	4	2	5	2	7	9	13	7	8
40-49 years	4	2	2	4	1	4	3	6	2	3
50-59 years	0	4	0	1	0	0	0	1	0	1
60+ years	0	0	0	0	0	0	0	0	0	0
TOTAL	33	32	21	33	31	35	38	49	38	35
All Prisoners										
14-16 years	38	41	24	21	26	16	26	49	42	23
17-20 years	425	411	371	347	360	424	334	336	326	316
21-29 years	709	630	622	598	601	696	620	601	609	590
30-39 years	274	252	214	239	206	277	287	309	296	305
40-49 years	91	82	64	86	75	94	75	95	116	114
50-59 years	29	30	22	23	33	29	21	40	31	35
60+ years	7	5	7	8	11	15	12	11	12	10
TOTAL	1573	1451	1324	1322	1312	1551	1375	1441	1432	1393

TABLE 6.9: Receptions under sentence of immediate custody, by offence 1988-1997

	1988	1989	1990	1991	1992	1993	1994	1995	1996	1997
Adult Males										
Violence against the person	217	205	219	228	188	344	266	263	235	214
Sexual offences	78	56	70	68	63	57	55	60	68	69
Burglary	191	155	145	120	106	144	117	120	113	112
Robbery	102	109	82	75	93	59	68	60	72	80
Theft	192	190	142	173	171	161	133	132	171	174
Fraud & forgery	46	46	35	44	36	48	35	54	49	36
Criminal damage	45	48	41	43	48	62	64	51	45	71
Drug offences	8	7	5	7	8	30	56	81	126	102
Motoring offences	116	89	111	88	99	116	133	122	99	111
Other offences	90	69	64	86	91	65	64	79	67	60
TOTAL	1085	974	914	932	903	1086	991	1022	1045	1029
Young Males										
Violence against the person	78	78	83	74	55	76	50	44	52	70
Sexual offences	8	13	18	7	9	8	4	6	11	4
Burglary	127	121	80	73	83	81	67	94	71	64
Robbery	35	35	25	36	35	30	29	23	22	25
Theft	72	77	61	67	66	47	43	51	90	75
Fraud & forgery	8	8	10	5	2	5	5	1	4	3
Criminal damage	44	36	28	30	29	55	27	21	33	26
Drug offences	1	0	0	0	2	14	10	21	23	16
Motoring offences	61	54	53	44	73	87	93	89	20	16
Other offences	21	23	31	21	24	27	18	20	23	30
TOTAL	455	445	389	357	378	430	346	370	349	329
Adult Females										
Violence against the person	3	2	4	4	10	7	9	3	1	3
Sexual offences	0	0	0	0	0	0	0	1	0	0
Burglary	0	1	0	0	1	0	2	1	0	2
Robbery	0	0	1	1	0	1	2	0	2	0
Theft	15	14	4	10	6	7	7	14	9	12
Fraud & forgery	3	6	2	3	1	3	1	6	1	2
Criminal damage	0	2	1	1	2	0	0	4	4	2
Drug offences	0	0	0	0	0	3	0	0	0	2
Motoring offences	0	0	0	2	0	0	2	3	1	0
Other offences	4	0	3	1	3	4	1	2	1	2
TOTAL	25	25	15	22	23	25	24	34	19	25
Young Females										
Violence against the person	2	2	1	3	3	5	2	2	7	3
Sexual offences	0	0	0	0	0	0	0	1	0	0
Burglary	0	2	0	0	1	1	2	0	1	2
Robbery	0	0	1	1	0	0	0	2	1	1
Theft	2	3	2	4	2	3	4	4	2	1
Fraud & forgery	1	0	0	0	0	0	2	1	0	0
Criminal damage	1	0	1	0	0	0	1	0	0	2
Drug offences	0	0	0	0	0	0	0	1	3	0
Motoring offences	0	0	0	1	1	1	0	0	2	0
Other offences	2	0	1	2	1	0	3	4	3	1
TOTAL	8	7	6	11	8	10	14	15	19	10

TABLE 6.10: Receptions under sentence of immediate custody, scheduled and non-scheduled offences 1988-1997

	1988	1989	1990	1991	1992	1993	1994	1995	1996	1997
Scheduled Offences										
Adult Male	347	349	320	362	342	466	386	379	338	356
Young Male	147	140	132	133	118	155	110	83	104	113
Adult Female	6	4	8	7	12	6	7	6	6	6
Young Female	2	3	4	4	3	3	3	5	7	6
TOTAL	502	496	464	506	475	630	506	473	455	481
Non-Scheduled Offences										
Adult Male	738	625	594	570	561	620	605	643	707	673
Young Male	308	305	257	224	260	275	236	287	245	216
Adult Female	19	21	7	15	11	19	17	28	13	19
Young Female	6	4	2	7	5	7	11	10	12	4
TOTAL	1071	955	860	816	837	921	869	968	977	912
OVERALL TOTAL	1573	1451	1324	1322	1312	1551	1375	1441	1432	1393

TABLE 6.11: Discharges from prison establishments, by type of prisoner 1988-1997

	1988	1989	1990	1991	1992	1993	1994	1995	1996	1997
Male Prisoners										
Remand										
Aged under 21	613	558	510	498	581	631	580	656	620	595
Aged 21 or over	1190	959	1097	1229	1272	1335	1301	1450	1508	1458
	1803	1517	1607	1727	1853	1966	1881	2106	2128	2053
Fine defaulter										
Aged under 21	446	337	295	341	356	337	269	341	365	350
Aged 21 or over	1441	1118	1225	1252	1314	1191	1139	1219	1321	1428
	1887	1455	1520	1593	1670	1528	1408	1560	1686	1778
Immediate Custody										
YOC	493	402	369	343	390	407	351	360	356	324
Young Prisoners	71	54	48	34	26	28	25	29	20	16
Adult Prisoners	1141	970	938	949	937	1038	1040	1096	1102	1087
	1705	1426	1355	1326	1353	1473	1416	1485	1478	1427
Non-Criminal	42	57	23	16	10	21	13	36	24	43
All Males	5437	4455	4505	4662	4886	4988	4718	5187	5316	5301
Female Prisoners										
Remand										
Aged under 21	20	25	21	27	32	19	47	27	35	34
Aged 21 or over	62	71	44	62	67	51	58	49	65	50
	82	96	65	89	99	70	105	76	100	84
Fine defaulter										
Aged under 21	10	7	14	12	7	18	9	8	11	12
Aged 21 or over	52	40	39	34	38	33	49	32	54	75
	62	47	53	46	45	51	58	40	65	87
Immediate Custody										
YOC	7	7	7	9	4	12	12	15	21	9
Young Prisoners	1	0	1	0	0	0	0	2	1	0
Adult Prisoners	31	23	13	24	15	28	25	35	18	31
	39	30	21	33	19	40	37	52	40	40
Non-Criminal	0	0	0	0	0	1	0	0	0	4
All Females	183	173	139	168	163	162	200	168	205	215
All Prisoners										
Remand	1885	1613	1672	1816	1952	2036	1986	2182	2228	2137
Fine Defaulter	1949	1502	1573	1639	1715	1579	1466	1600	1751	1865
Immediate Custody	1744	1456	1376	1359	1372	1513	1453	1537	1518	1467
Non-Criminal	42	57	23	16	10	22	13	36	24	47
TOTAL	5620	4628	4644	4830	5049	5150	4918	5355	5521	5516

Notes: (1)   Figures shown for the YOC relate to sentences to the YOC establishment. For administrative reasons, the male figures may not equate precisely with the number of persons placed in YOC Hydebank.

Coverage of notifiable and indictable offences

1. In England and Wales classification of offences recorded by the police is based on a list of 'notifiable offences' which the Home Office requires to be notified by the various police forces. A separate, similar, but slightly different list of 'indictable offences' is issued for classifying the more serious offences which are the subject of court proceedings ('indictable offences' are essentially those for which proceedings can or must be heard in the Crown Court - see Appendix 2).

2. In Northern Ireland the classification systems used for both offences recorded by the police and court proceedings are broadly similar to those in use in England and Wales. The same terminology is used, though some differences do occur, largely because of differences in legislation. Column 1 of the table overleaf comprises a list of offences grouped under 11 main headings. By reference to this list columns 2 and 3 indicate the approximate coverage of notifiable and indictable offences for England and Wales, and for Northern Ireland. Generally, attempting, conspiring, inciting, abetting, causing or permitting a crime is included with the crime itself, though in some cases it is shown separately.

3. The terms 'theft', 'burglary', and 'robbery' are often confused. They can be defined as follows:

(a) Theft: The dishonest appropriation of another's property with the intention of permanently depriving the owner of it.

(b) Burglary: Entering a building as a trespasser with the intention of committing theft, rape, grievous bodily harm or unlawful damage. If a person commits the above offence whilst in possession of a weapon, or explosive the offence becomes aggravated burglary for which the maximum penalty is imprisonment for life.

(c) Robbery: The use or threat of force to a person immediately before or at the time of theft.

OFFENCE CATEGORY	NOTIFIABLE OFFENCES	INDICTABLE OFFENCES
I Violence against the person		
Murder	The following are excluded in both	All are included in both E&W and N.I.
Attempted murder	E&W and N.I.	A specific offence of intimidation is
Threat or conspiracy to murder	-Manslaughter due to diminished	included in N.I.
Manslaughter	responsibility.	
Infanticide	-Cruelty to or neglect of children.	
Child destruction	-Some acts endangering life at sea.	
Causing death by reckless driving		
Manslaughter due to diminished responsibility		
Wounding or other act endangering life	A specific offence of intimidation is included in N.I.	
Endangering railway passenger		
Endangering life at sea		
Other wounding etc.		
Assault		
Cruelty to or neglect of children		
Abandoning child under two years		
Child abduction		
Procuring illegal abortion		
Concealment of birth		
II Sexual offences	Soliciting by a man is excluded in both E&W and N.I.	All included in both E&W and N.I.
III Burglary	Going equipped for stealing is counted in the 'other indictable' category in E&W, but as burglary in N.I.	All included in both E&W and N.I.
IV Robbery	In N.I. includes the specific offence of 'hijacking'.	In N.I. includes the specific offence of 'hijacking'.

V	Theft and handling stolen goods	All included in both E&W and N.I.	All included in both E&W and N.I.
VI	Fraud & forgery	Offences relating to bankruptcy are all excluded in E&W but only some in N.I.	Copyright offences are included in N.I. In E&W they are classified as 'other indictable'.
VII	Criminal Damage	In England and Wales all criminal damage offences are in theory covered. In N.I. coverage is restricted to offences where damage exceeds £200.	Offences where damage is less than £400 are summary in nature, but are included in N.I.
VIII	Other indictable offences (non-motoring) Drug offences Blackmail Kidnapping	Includes 'going equipped for stealing' in E&W. Most offences from 'betting, gaming and lotteries' onwards are excluded in both E&W and N.I. Some minor differences in coverage occur.	Some differences in coverage arise between E&W and N.I. because of legislative differences.
		'Treason', 'riot', 'unlawful assembly' and 'other offences against the state' are presented as a separate category in N.I.	'Treason', 'riot', 'unlawful assembly' and 'other offences against the state' are presented as a separate category in N.I.
		Some summary offences are included (see below).	
IX	Indictable motoring offences Reckless driving offences Driving licence offences Operator's licence Vehicle insurance offences Vehicle registration and licensing offences Driver's work record and employment offences Vehicle testing offences	Excluded in both E&W and N.I.	Only a single category of motoring offences (indictable and summary) is identified in N.I.

X	**Summary offences (non-motoring)**	Almost all are excluded in both	In E&W and N.I. summary criminal
	Aggravated assault	E&W and N.I. summary criminal	damage offences are included with
	Assault on a constable	damage cases in E&W and N.I. are	indictable offences. A small number
	Brothel keeping	included with indictable offences.	of 'other' offences are also included
	Cruelty to a child		as indictable in both E&W and N.I.
	Interference with motor vehicle	A few other offences are included	
	Indecent exposure	under the heading 'Other notifiable	Some difference in coverage occurs
	Summary offences of criminal	offences'.	between E&W and N.I. because of
	or malicious damage		legislative differences.
	Unlawful possession		
	Found in enclosed premises		
	Summary drug offences		
	Summary immigration offences		
	Impersonating a police officer		

XI	**Summary offences (Motoring)**	Miscellaneous summary motoring	All excluded in both E&W and N.I.
	Unfit to drive through drink or	offences.	
	drugs		Only a single category of motoring
	Racing reckless driving		offences (indictable and summary)
	Speeding - road limits		is identified in N.I. at present.
	Speeding - vehicle limits		
	Motorway offences (excluding speeding)		
	Careless driving		
	Playstreet offences		
	Prohibited driving		
	Neglect of traffic directions		
	Obstruction (waiting and parking		
	place offences)		
	Lighting offences		
	Vehicle or part in dangerous		
	condition. Vehicle or part in		
	defective condition. Trailer		
	offences		
	Motor Cycle offences		
	Load offences		
	Noise offences		
	Driving licence offences		

Vehicle insurance offences

**Vehicle registration and licensing
(Excise) offences**

**Work record and employment
offences**

Accident offences

**Vehicle testing offences and
proscribed goods vehicle testing
and planting offences**

The criminal courts in Northern Ireland

General

1. Some crimes are obviously less serious than others. Less serious criminal offences are dealt with by way of summary trial in a magistrates' court (sometimes referred to as a Court of petty sessions). These offences include assaults, minor offences of dishonesty, (theft, handling stolen goods and deception) and offences against the Road Traffic (Northern Ireland) Order 1981. The trial takes place before a Resident Magistrate sitting alone, there is no jury, the Magistrate decides issues of law and fact, and on conviction passes sentence.

Scheduled Offences

2. The more serious crimes like murder, robbery and rape are tried on indictment in the Crown Court by a judge and jury; though initially committal proceedings will also have been heard in the magistrates' court, where the Magistrate decides if there is sufficient evidence to merit the accused being sent for trial. In the Crown Court the judge decides all issues of law but questions of fact are left to be resolved by the jury who will decide whether or not the accused is guilty of the offence with which he is charged. The judge of course will pass sentence if the accused is convicted.

3. Paragraphs 1 and 2 outline the two main forms of procedure and trial. In Northern Ireland, however, since 1973 a special procedure has developed for dealing with serious offences relating to terrorism, based on recommendations of a Commission under Lord Diplock. The majority of these offences are also tried in the Crown Court on indictment but they are tried under procedures and rules of evidence which have been modified. The most important difference is that they are tried by a judge without a jury, the judge alone deciding all issues of fact as well as law, and passing sentence after conviction. The offences triable in this way are listed in Schedule 1 of the Northern Ireland (Emergency Provisions) Act 1996 and are referred to as 'scheduled' offences. The special non-jury Crown Courts are often referred to as 'Diplock' courts.

4. Some of the offences listed in Schedule 1 of the 1996 Act may be de-scheduled by the Attorney General certifying in a particular case that the offence is not to be treated as a scheduled offence. They should be de-scheduled if no element of terrorism was involved in their commission, but if the Attorney General refuses to de-schedule an offence there is no appeal against this decision. An example of an offence which should be de-scheduled is murder where it occurs in a domestic setting and is clearly unconnected with terrorist activity. Other offences are to be treated as scheduled only in particular circumstances, i.e. robbery, only where it is charged that an explosive, firearm, imitation firearm or weapon of offence was used in its commission. Some offences can never be de-scheduled; these include causing grievous bodily harm by explosives, withholding information about acts of terrorism and other offences clearly linked with terrorism by their very nature.

Triable-either-way Offences

5. Whilst certain less serious offences, known as summary offences, must always be tried in a magistrates' court; and certain of the most serious offences, known as indictable offences must always be heard in the Crown Court; there is a third category of triable-either-way offences which, under one of three sets of circumstances, can be tried either in a magistrates' court or the Crown Court.

(a) Some offences normally tried summarily can be tried on indictment if the offence is one for which a person, if convicted, can be sent to prison for more than 6 months; and the defendant opts to be tried on indictment.

(b) Some offences which are normally tried on indictment can be tried summarily if the Magistrate considers that the case is not a serious one of its type and it is expedient to deal with it summarily; and the accused and the prosecution both agree to a summary trial. Petty theft and some types of assault fall into this category.

(c) In many cases the statute which creates a crime expressly states that it can be tried summarily or on indictment. It is then up to the prosecution bearing in mind the seriousness of the individual case, to decide which form of trial to use.

6. The mode of trial of scheduled offences depends on the general rules above, i.e. whether or not the offence is one which must be tried on indictment in the Crown Court or is a triable-either-way offence which will be tried summarily if the appropriate conditions are fulfilled. None of the scheduled offences fall into the category which must be tried summarily. Scheduled offences to be tried in the Crown Court are tried by a judge sitting alone without a jury. If they are dealt with in the magistrates' court the procedure is the same as that for non-scheduled summary offences.

Magistrates' Courts

7. The vast majority of all criminal offences dealt with in Northern Ireland are tried summarily in a magistrates' court. Over half of these offences are offences against the Road Traffic (NI) Order 1981. It is estimated that where the defendant has a choice between summary trial and trial on indictment, approximately 3 out of 4 cases are dealt with summarily. This is mainly because this mode of trial is much quicker and the sentencing powers of a Magistrate are more restricted than those of a Crown Court judge - the most serious punishment which a Magistrate can impose is 12 months in prison, unless consecutive terms of imprisonment are imposed for more than one offence, when the limit is extended to 18 months.

8. The defendant has a right to appeal against his conviction or the sentence imposed upon him or both. The appeal takes place in the County Court before a County Court judge sitting without a jury. If the appeal is against conviction the accused will get a complete rehearing of his case. If the appeal is against sentence only the judge will review the sentence imposed by the Magistrate and affirm, reduce or increase it.

9. Appeals on a point of law from either the County Court or the magistrates' court go to the Court of Appeal. The Court of Appeal's ruling may be further challenged in the House of Lords, with leave from the Court of Appeal or the House of Lords.

Crown Court

10. Trial on indictment in the Crown Court follows after the accused has been returned for trial at committal proceedings in a magistrates' court. The Department of Public Prosecutions prepares a formal document called an indictment stating the charges which the accused will face. The matters are then tried before a judge sitting with a jury or if the offences are 'scheduled offences' sitting without a jury.

11. The Crown Court sits at nine different places throughout the province and trial of non-scheduled offences take place at the sitting of the Crown Court determined by the Magistrate who committed the accused, usually the Crown Court acting for the County Court division in which the offence is alleged to have been committed. All 'scheduled' offences are heard at the Crown Court sitting in Belfast.

12. Appeal from the Crown Court is to the Court of Appeal. The defendant can appeal on a point of law without obtaining the permission of any court. If he wishes to appeal against conviction on a question of fact he needs the permission of either the Crown Court judge or the Court of Appeal. If he wishes to appeal against sentence he needs the leave of the Court of Appeal.

13. All persons convicted of a scheduled offence tried on indictment can appeal against conviction to the Court of Appeal on any ground and without leave. This automatic right of appeal is a safeguard built into the system because in these cases there is no jury.

14. The prosecution has no right to appeal against the acquittal of a defendant who has been tried on indictment. The Attorney-General can refer a point of law to the Court of Appeal for its opinion, but even if the Court of Appeal considers that the trial judge made an error of law resulting in an acquittal, the acquittal still stands. The reference and subsequent ruling is useful in guiding the prosecution of future trials.

15. Further appeal by the defence or prosecution lies to the House of Lords. As with summary trials the leave of either the Court of Appeal or the House of Lords is required.

| *Juvenile Court* |

16. The Juvenile Court is a special magistrates' court constituted to deal with proceedings against children between the ages of 10 and 16. The Juvenile Court operates along broadly similar lines to the adult court, but with some differences:

(a) It consists of a bench of three members, of whom the chairman is a Resident Magistrate.

(b) Proceedings are held in private. Only persons connected with the case and court officials are present.

(c) The Juvenile Court can deal summarily with any indictable offence other than murder if it thinks that such a course is expedient and if the prosecution and the child's parents or the young person consents. It can make an order which might have been made by the Crown Court had the matter been tried on indictment.

(d) In addition to hearing criminal proceedings the court also hears proceedings relating to the care, protection and control of juveniles, though when a juvenile is charged jointly with an adult, charges will initially be heard in the ordinary magistrates' court.

Sentences available to the court

1. The types of sentence available to courts in Northern Ireland have evolved over the years with legislative change. Those available are outlined below. Sentencing to prison, Young Offenders' Centre or a training school are collectively referred to as custodial disposals; probation orders, community service orders and attendance centre orders are collectively referred to as supervision orders.

Imprisonment

2. Imprisonment is the most severe penalty ordinarily available to the courts. The length of a term of imprisonment is determined either by statute or a judge or Magistrate in a common law case. It can vary from a few days to life, which is mandatory for a person convicted of murder. In Northern Ireland the maximum length of sentence that can be given by a Magistrate is 12 months for an indictable offence or 18 months if the person is convicted of more than one indictable offence.

3. Imprisonment is a sentence mostly confined to persons aged 21 and over (see Young Offenders' Centre); but there is provision for detention of persons under 21 in a prison where the circumstances warrant it. Such detention is included in the statistics of imprisonment and can be for a stipulated sentence of over 4 years or at the Secretary of State's pleasure - analogous to a life sentence for persons under 18 when their crime was committed.

4. Prison sentences are rarely served in full. Remission may be granted at up to 50% of the sentence depending upon the circumstances, and 'lifers' may be released on licence at the decision of the Secretary of State. In murder cases the Secretary of State must consult the Lord Chief Justice and trial judge (if available).

Young Offenders' *Centre*

5. Sentencing to the Young Offenders' Centre is instead of imprisonment for persons under 21 who have been given custodial sentences of up to 4 years.

Training School *Order*

6. Training schools are residential establishments approved under Section 137 of the Children and Young Persons Act (Northern Ireland) 1968 for the reception and training of children and young persons. They are also registered as remand homes. Duration of stay is determined by the Act but school managers have discretion to release persons on licence. The duration of stay may be up to 2 years in the case of someone under the age of 16. Persons over 16 may be detained until the age of 19. Some individuals attend the school on a daily basis only.

Suspended Sentence

7. This is a deterrent sentence, the term of which must not exceed 2 years. The period of suspension is between 1 and 3 years. If, during the suspension period, the offender commits an offence punishable by imprisonment, the court may order the suspended sentence (or a lesser term) to take effect. The court may also decide to impose a new suspension period or make no order with respect of the suspended sentence.

Community Service *Order*

8. This Order requires the offender to do unpaid work in the community. It can be given to someone aged 16 or over convicted of an imprisonable offence if the offender consents and may be between 40 and 240 hours duration.

Attendance Centre Order	9. This Order deprives male juvenile offenders of some of their leisure time. This is usually a Saturday morning. It avoids removal from the home environment for extended periods.
Probation	10. The probation period may last for a period between 6 months to 3 years. It puts the offender under the supervision of a social worker and is not a punishment but a period during which probation personnel act as a source of guidance to avoid re-offending.
Fine	11. This is a financial punishment, the maximum level of which is generally set by statute. At common law the amount is unlimited. It is not a part of the principle of this sentence to fine a wealthy person according to their means. But it is thought desirable for the Magistrate to have some knowledge of the financial circumstances of the offender.
Deferred Sentence	12. After conviction, a person may have the sentence deferred for a period of up to 6 months. Sentence is passed after changes (if any) in the circumstances of the case have been assessed. For example, the offender may have made some form of reparation.
Recognizance	13. This is called being 'bound over' and may be either 'bound over on own recognizance' or 'to keep the peace' or 'bound over on probation' etc. The offender and/or guarantors may enter into sureties which may be forfeited if the person re-offends.
Conditional Discharge	14. This Order imposes a condition upon the offender, i.e. that the offender commits no further offence for a specified period (1 to 3 years). If the condition is broken, the person may be dealt with for the earlier and the current offence.
Absolute Discharge	15. This may be imposed where punishment is considered inappropriate. The offender while found guilty is not further liable for the offence.

Other Publications

A series of statistical bulletins may be obtained from Statistics and Research Branch, Northern Ireland Office, Massey House, Stoney Road, Belfast. The series includes:

The Court of Appeal in Northern Ireland
STATISTICS & RESEARCH BULLETIN 1/95

The Use of the Fine in Northern Ireland
STATISTICS & RESEARCH BULLETIN 2/95

Statistics on the Police and Criminal Evidence (NI) Order 1989
STATISTICS & RESEARCH FACT SHEET 1/95

Northern Ireland Security Statistics 1994
STATISTICS & RESEARCH FACT SHEET 2/95

Experience of Drugs in Northern Ireland: Preliminary Research Findings from the 1994/5 Northern Ireland Crime Survey
RESEARCH FINDINGS 1/96

Fear of Crime and Likelihood of Victimisation in Northern Ireland
RESEARCH FINDINGS 2/96

Juveniles and the Northern Ireland Criminal Justice System

Criminal Justice in Northern Ireland. Key Statistics 1996
A NORTHERN IRELAND OFFICE CRIME FACT CARD

Sexual Offending in Northern Ireland
A NORTHERN IRELAND OFFICE CRIME FACT CARD

Changing Patterns of Drug Use in Northern Ireland - Some Recent Survey Findings
RESEARCH FINDINGS 1/97

Gender and the Northern Ireland Criminal Justice System

Drugs in Northern Ireland. Some Key Facts 1997

The Use of Bail and Levels of Offending on Bail in Northern Ireland
RESEARCH FINDINGS 1/98

Digest of Information on the Northern Ireland Criminal Justice System - 3

Printed in the United Kingdom for the Stationery Office Limited
Dd 601838 C3 5/98 Gp 7439